THE MYSTERIES OF THE ROSARY

THE MYSTERIES OF THE ROSARY:

Mirror of Scripture and Gateway to Prayer

DEACON ROY BARKLEY

ALBA·HOUSE   NEW·YORK

SOCIETY OF ST. PAUL, 2187 VICTORY BLVD., STATEN ISLAND, NEW YORK 10314

ST PAULS

Library of Congress Cataloging-in-Publication Data

Barkley, Roy.
   The mysteries of the rosary: mirror of scripture and gateway to prayer / Roy Barkley.
     p. cm.
   Includes bibliographical references.
   ISBN 0-8189-0848-3 (alk. paper)
    1. Mysteries of the Rosary. 2. Catholic Church—Prayer-books and devotions—
English. I. Title.

BT303.B255 2000
242'.74—dc21

                                       00-032781

Produced and designed in the United States of America by the
Fathers and Brothers of the Society of St. Paul,
2187 Victory Boulevard, Staten Island, New York 10314-6603,
as part of their communications apostolate.

ISBN: 0-8189-0848-3

Printing Information:

Current Printing - first digit   1   2   3   4   5   6   7   8   9   10

Year of Current Printing - first year shown

2001   2002   2003   2004   2005   2006   2007   2008   2009   2010

TABLE OF CONTENTS

PREFACE

*T*his book results from more than twenty years of devotion to the Blessed Virgin. My main purpose in it is to encourage the use of the Rosary as the centerpiece, next to the Mass, of one's prayer life. Its subject is the connections between the Mysteries of the Rosary and the rest of Scripture, and between the Rosary and some of those elements in our culture that plead most insistently for a remedy from the Mother of God. My purpose is to lead the reader to a more profound devotion to Mary and through her to Jesus Christ. That devotion in turn should lead to an enriched understanding of the spiritual needs of our culture, which cry out for conversion. The reader's prayer and fasting, offered to the Savior through the Immaculate Heart of Mary, will bear abundant fruit for the kingdom of heaven.

The main chapters—chapters two through four, on the Joyful, Sorrowful, and Glorious Mysteries of the Rosary—share an internal structure marked by boldface headings. The first section on each mystery is devoted to an explication of the literal meaning of the Scripture in which the mystery occurs. The second is about some of the most important affiliations between that passage and the rest of the Bible. The third is a reflection on the application of the mystery to one's individual spiritual life, and to cultural analysis and current problems. Understanding the application of Scripture to life is a responsibility of each Christian and part of his vocation to prayer. The fourth section briefly recalls the role of the Blessed Virgin in these scenes from the life of Christ. And the fifth offers suggested intentions for which one might offer a given decade of the Rosary. Although these intentions are mere suggestions, designed to lead to further meditation and prayer, most of them have developed logically in my own prayer life from the content of the mystery.

My method in this book is *loosely* derived from the exegetical method of St. Augustine, who wrote of the literal, allegorical, moral, and anagogical meanings of Scripture. I intend in these pages to supply a wealth of scriptural detail and broad contexts that is often neglected. The chapter structure is in accord with the threefold process of contemplation of the mysteries, as I see it: (1) understanding their meaning, both in their immediate context and in the context of relevant other passages of Scripture, (2) applying that meaning to one's own spiritual life (especially by scriptural reflection and prayer), and (3) becoming a channel of the grace suggested by that meaning to others through prayer, inner conversion, and continual self-offering. The Blessed Virgin will constantly accompany anyone who submits to her guidance in such reflection and prayer.

The incidents in the life of Christ called the Mysteries of the Rosary summarize the story of our redemption. They are all derived either directly or indirectly from Sacred Scripture. All but the last two come straight from the inspired word, whereas the Assumption and the Coronation of the Blessed Virgin are prophetically veiled in Scripture and subsequently elaborated in authoritative Sacred Tradition, which reflects the contemplative and Spirit-guided mind of the Church. In fact, the mysteries embody in small compass so much of the meaning of God's word that they almost constitute a summary of revelation. The Visitation, for instance, does not occur in isolation but in a rich cultural and spiritual context. In its content it reverberates with the messianic prophecies of the Old Testament. In form its poetry reflects a genealogy in the Old Testament canticles. In its application to the Christian life, it embodies and enjoins the humble submission to God for which all of his servants should strive. The Visitation and its great canticle, the *Magnificat*, therefore echo salvation history from the beginning to the present. The same can be said of the other mysteries.

Mary's brightness is a reflected light. In the *Catechism of the Catholic Church*, the most monumental exercise of the Magisterium since the Second Vatican Council, the Church teaches that "What the Catholic faith believes about Mary is based on what it believes about Christ, and what it teaches about Mary illumines in turn its faith in Christ."[1] The Gospel of St. John informs us, for instance, that from the cross Jesus gave Mary to John as the latter's adoptive mother. Because of the Son of God all human beings are brothers and sisters, and the Lord is their brother. Mary's motherhood originated in the mind of God. The brotherhood of all men has a similar origin. It results from the Incarnation, the great redemptive act of God's mercy. In contemplation of that motherhood and that brotherhood, the Church extends the Virgin's maternity to the whole human race. Mary is Mother of us all. St. John's filial regard for Mary thus becomes ours; we know her as our Mother, given to us by the Lord. But we also observe the death of Jesus and its meaning through the eyes of the Virgin, who, for her part, saw in this spiritual adoption the great love of her firstborn Son for all the beneficiaries of his Passion, including the ancients and those yet unborn. All are her children because all belong to God, who gave them to her. Thus Mary's light, like all true human understanding, comes from God and proclaims its source.

A book about the mysteries is therefore a scriptural, Christ-centered, and Marian book. Many books have been written about

---

[1] *Catechism of the Catholic Church*, 487.

Mary, most notably the works of St. Louis de Montfort, which are uniquely excellent aids to Marian devotion. The footnotes of the present book are intended to indicate the source of material used and to point to further reading. Although I have made no attempt to multiply secondary references, I have sought, particularly in Chapter 1, to indicate the magisterial history of my observations. Most readers will readily see that other works could have been cited. My goal is, again, to encourage devotion to the Blessed Virgin and to bring her bountiful influence to bear on the world we live in, not to provide a Marian bibliography.

New Testament quotations in this book are for the most part from the St. Paul Catholic Edition of the New Testament (New York, ST PAULS/Alba House; Boston, Pauline Books and Media); all other biblical quotations are from the Revised Standard Version (Ignatius Press) unless otherwise indicated.

THE MYSTERIES OF THE ROSARY

Chapter One

MARY AND THE ROSARY

Let us give thanks to God for his great bounty in all things, especially for giving us the Blessed Virgin Mary, the mysteries of the holy Rosary, and the great salvation that they epitomize, which is brought to us by our gracious Lady's *fiat*.

1

(a) The Mirror

Mary and the Word. How much of Christianity stands upon those New Testament scenes that are the subjects of the Rosary! How wonderful it is that the Catholic Church, guided by the Holy Spirit, has seen the centrality of these mysteries and made them such a rich part of her scriptural and spiritual heritage! How insightful have been the Church Fathers, the popes, the doctors of the Church, her loyal theologians, and her innumerable children in perceiving the true significance of Mary, the Handmaid of the Lord! For it is in the light of Mary's maternal concern that the salvific events of Christ's life come most near to us ordinary Catholics. She was his first and most avid disciple, and the Scriptures enable us to be with her in his presence. With her we reflect upon the unfathomable mercy of God, who gave us Christ for our Savior. With her we reflect upon the agonizing demands of the Redeemer's mission, which are the culminating events of Scripture. With her we see the glory of the risen Christ, and in her exaltation we see writ large our own destiny in him.

The overwhelming importance of the mysteries to the entire Christian story is nowhere better illustrated than in the Resurrection. The Resurrection of Christ draws all of Scripture to itself, as the risen Christ draws all of mankind. The Resurrection of Jesus is the pinnacle of Scripture—indeed, of world history. It proves the truth of the doctrine of the general resurrection, which was gradually revealed in Old Testament times—in the Psalms, in the book of Daniel, in Wisdom, in the Maccabees. By the time of Christ this doctrine had become the common property of such orthodox Jewish sects as the Pharisees, from which St. Paul springs. (It was to be sure still controversial; some didn't believe in it. Some still don't.) The Resurrection also establishes Christ's eternal primacy. St. Paul calls attention to how Christ's victory over death demonstrates both the inevitability of the general resurrection and the validity of the apostolic preaching (1 Corinthians 15:12-23). Furthermore, the Resurrection is the chief topic in the early Church, for the apostles knew how much depended upon it. The empty tomb demonstrates with great finality the divinity of Christ, and in doing so it validates his origins and indicates the source of his miraculous powers. It tells us that he arose physically; otherwise the absence of his body from the tomb would have meant nothing. The Resurrection tells us also that Jesus has the power to save. It is therefore the lynchpin of the apostles' faith. They knew about it at first hand, for they were eyewitnesses to the risen Jesus, with whom they conversed and broke bread. In addition, the Resurrection is the necessary antecedent to St. John's apocalyptic vision in the book of Revelation. The Resurrection demonstrates conclusively that Jesus is the Messiah. The Resurrection inspires the Church's retrospective understanding of the Scriptures, and especially of the Messianic traditions embodied in them. In fact, the Resurrection *mirrors* the Scriptures all the way from the Protevangelium, or Proto-Gospel, in Genesis 3[1] to the vision of Judgment Day in Revelation. The Resurrection is the hinge of Christianity. It is also a mystery of the Rosary, which draws all of Scripture to itself.

Pope Paul VI, in his great Marian document *Marialis Cultus*, remarks upon how

> ...the orderly and gradual unfolding of the Rosary *reflects* the very way in which the Word of God, mercifully entering into human affairs, brought about the Redemption. The Rosary considers in harmonious succession the principal salvific events accomplished in Christ, from his virginal

---

[1] God tells the serpent, "I will put enmity between you and the woman, and between your seed and her seed; he shall bruise your head, and you shall bruise his heel." Thus Genesis prophesies that the seed of Mary, the antitype of Eve, will crush the serpent of evil and overcome the effect of sin, which is death. Jesus accomplished this victory by rising from the dead.

conception and the mysteries of his childhood to the culminating moments of the Passover—the blessed passion and the glorious resurrection—and to the effects of this on the infant Church on the day of Pentecost, and on the Virgin Mary when at the end of her earthly life she was assumed body and soul into her heavenly home.... [T]he division of the mysteries of the Rosary into three parts not only adheres strictly to the chronological order of the facts but above all *reflects* the plan of the original proclamation of the Faith and sets forth once more the mystery of Christ in the very way in which it is seen by Saint Paul in the celebrated "hymn" of the Letter to the Philippians— kenosis, death and exaltation (Philippians 2:5-11).[2]

All of the mysteries except the last two, the Assumption and the Coronation of the Virgin, are drawn directly from New Testament stories of the life of Christ. The last two are implied in Scripture and elaborated in Sacred Tradition by an inescapable logic that stood unquestioned until the Protestant Reformation. The contemplative subjects of the Rosary are thus solidly grounded in Scripture—not in obscure or secondary events, but in the principal saving acts related by the inspired authors. It is for this reason that Pope Pius XI called the Rosary the "Breviary of the Gospel and of Christian Life."[3]

So the mysteries mirror the Scriptures. But what of Mary herself? What advantage is gained by seeing all these Gospel events through the same Marian lens? In a sense, this entire book is an answer to that question. More narrowly speaking, however—addressing the relation of Mary to the central scriptural events—one *is impelled* by faith in the Scriptures to include her, to stand by her

---

[2] Pope Paul VI, *Marialis Cultus* (Apostolic Exhortation for the Right Ordering and Development of Devotion to the Blessed Virgin Mary), February 2, 1974, no. 45. Italics added.

[3] Pope Pius XI, *Ingravescentibus Malis* (Encyclical on the Rosary), September 29, 1937, no. 9.

side and observe, to feel the force of these scenes from the life of her divine Son with her. This is so because she was chosen by God, prepared by God, called by God not only to *be* there, but to fulfill an absolutely unique vocation with regard to our salvation. Who else is with the Lord throughout his life? Because of her generous, grace-filled response to God's call, Christ himself came into the world. If we wish to be there in contemplation, to witness his coming, we will be in the presence of his Mother. If we wish to find him in the Temple, to watch him turn water into wine, to share the anxious pain of his disciples during his final night of trial, to stand at the foot of the cross, we will be in the presence of his Mother. If we wish to see his empty tomb we will be with his Mother, for she is there. If we want to witness the descent of the Paraclete on Pentecost, we will wait with Mary and the apostles. No other biblical person is with the Lord throughout his life and mission. Mary alone had this privilege.

Because of the centrality of her role, she is foreshadowed in prophecy in the Old Testament and becomes the antitype of which Eve is the type. Eve fell to sin, while Mary remained pure. Eve gave the serpent power over her children, while Mary through her Child destroys the force of sin. As the headwaters of the Old Covenant rise in Eden, so those of the New Covenant rise in Mary, the enclosed and inviolate Garden of the Holy Spirit. In union with her Son, she is the protagonist of the messianic story. Though she is the Handmaid or servant of the Messiah, she plays an emphatically pivotal role in his mission. It is through her consent that the serpent's head is crushed.[4]

---

[4] See Pope Pius IX, *Ineffabilis Deus* (Apostolic Constitution Proclaiming the Immaculate Conception), December 8, 1854, on "Mary Compared With Eve" and Pope Pius XII, *Ad Caeli Reginam* (Encyclical Proclaiming the Queenship of Mary), October 11, 1954, no. 38. The latter teaches: "[A]s Christ, the new Adam, must be called a King not merely because He is Son of God, but also because He is our Redeemer, so, analogously, the Most Blessed Virgin is queen not only because she is Mother of God, but also because, as the new Eve, she was associated with the new Adam."

For this reason the Fathers found many types—or figurative foreshadowings—of the Blessed Virgin in the Old Testament. They saw prophecies of her in Noah's ark, in which mankind was saved from destruction; in Jacob's ladder, which gave access to heaven; in the bush that indicated Yahweh's presence to Moses—which, though burning, was not consumed—just as Mary's virginity was not destroyed by God's coming as Christ; and in many other figures.[5] Mary is a new and perfect Judith, who delivers God's people from their enemies. In her childbearing she recalls Hannah, mother of Samuel, whose canticle is a powerful analogue of the *Magnificat*. Mary herself is therefore a mirror of Scripture.

Vocation of the Blessed Virgin. The teaching of the Church in the Second Vatican Council and afterward insists that everyone has a unique calling. No longer does the word *vocation* apply only to the calling of clergymen and religious. Strictly speaking, of course, this has always been the case, though in common usage the emphasis is new. The idea has been latent, or even explicit, in the Church's teaching since her beginning. St. Francis de Sales, for instance, in the *Introduction to the Devout Life*, writes of how each person in his sphere of life is called to serve the Lord.

Although no two vocations are alike in concrete details, Mary had a very special vocation indeed, to which she responded with utterly singular devotion. Meditation upon her vocation and how she fulfilled it is a vital part of understanding the Rosary and the Virgin's part in the plan of salvation. She was *called* to cooperate most intimately with the Holy Spirit in bringing God the Son into the world, and in serving as the principal handmaid to his mission. For this sublime task she was selected from the beginning of the world and especially prepared. In particular, she was miraculously

---

[5] See Pope Pius IX, *Ineffabilis Deus*, on "Interpreters of the Sacred Scripture."

exempted from the stain of original sin so that she could be a fitting vessel to bear him into the world. The Holy Father wrote in 1661,

> Concerning the most Blessed Virgin Mary, Mother of God, ancient indeed is that devotion of the faithful based on the belief that her soul, in the first instant of its creation … was, by a special grace and privilege of God, in view of the merits of Jesus Christ, her Son and the Redeemer of the human race, preserved free from all stain of original sin.[6]

Because this doctrine was held "in all times and places" throughout the history of the Apostolic Church, and because the time was right, Pope Pius IX defined the Immaculate Conception as a dogma of the Catholic faith. The stage was set by her freedom from original sin for Mary's calling and her gracious response—in other words, for her *vocation*. In every aspect of God's call, she freely answered not only with submission, which is passive though it may be deliberately chosen, but with a determined will to cooperate actively.

The Blessed Virgin's vocation, as she lived (and lives) it, comprised her lifelong *fiat* to all of God's requests; her deliberate, unswerving orientation toward the Son of God and his interests, in which she lived under her own admonition, "Do whatever he tells you"; and her continued care, after his Ascension, for all her children—especially after she was called to his side in the Assumption. Much of this book is about the vocation of the Virgin and how she lived it. But because the subject is specifically discussed so little—and because it forms a background to the entire Rosary—its salient features need treatment here.

---

[6] Pope Alexander VII, quoted in *Ineffabilis Deus* under the heading "The Roman Doctrine."

Mary's lifelong *fiat* begins even before the archangel Gabriel appears to her with his astonishing announcement and addresses her as "full of grace" (Luke 1:28). She has already, it is traditionally said, consecrated herself to God. She is already in prayer when the angel arrives. She has already said "let it be" to the Creator's will. Her spiritual life has prepared her for the moment of God's great call. Then when the angel speaks, she is ready to respond to God's stupendous request with *Fiat mihi secundum verbum tuum*— "Let it be done to me as you say." This *fiat*, enshrined in the mystery of the Annunciation and in the *Angelus*, was therefore not just a momentary consent. It was, to be sure, Mary's freely given agreement to the Incarnation through her own body.[7] But it was much more than that. It was a consent to assume the *entire range of obligations* that went along with having *this particular Son*. It comprehended her role in all the scenes of Scripture, from the Annunciation itself to her exaltation in the stars as described in the book of Revelation. But it also comprehended all of *his* interests, which were the entire unfolding story of man's redemption. It was Mary's *vocation* to lay the Son of God in a manger, to care for him in his childhood, to persuade him to begin his ministry of miraculous signs at Cana (John 1), to suffer ever more acutely with him as she pondered the nature and cost of his mission, to comfort and help the apostles as they waited for the descent of the Holy Spirit, and, after her passage from this life (often referred to as her dormition) and exaltation, to look with loving care upon everyone whose salvation he had purchased. In order to fulfill this great calling, Mary lived a life of chosen self-denial and of absolute purity of body and intellect. She started immaculate, she stayed immaculate. Had she not done so, as Pope Pius XII teaches,[8] the "enmity" between her

---

[7] Pope Leo XIII, *Octobri Mense*, September 22, 1891, no. 4.
[8] Pope Pius XII, *Fulgens Corona*, September 8, 1953, no. 7.

and the serpent would have been fatally compromised. She would have been, like Eve, a partner rather than an implacable enemy of the serpent. This complicity would have disqualified her from bearing the Son of God. It would have falsified the prophecy of the Protevangelium, in which the Church sees the Immaculate Conception foreshadowed.

We children of Mary should be aware of the great example her *fiat* sets for us, especially in decisive moments of life. In little matters as well as great ones, we should constantly strive to know and accept God's will. But this is especially true when we choose a state of life, with all the commitments it entails, or enter into some other lifelong, vocational commitment. When a Catholic couple stand before the altar and express their consent to love and honor each other until death, they are echoing the Blessed Virgin's permanent acceptance of God's will. When one is confirmed, or when a man receives the sacrament of Holy Orders, Mary's *fiat* is again voiced. We often hear that the sacraments, especially the "state of life" sacraments, have an ontological significance. They change our relation to the whole of existence. They change our very being. A married person, for instance, is not simply a single person with something added, but a different kind of person with different obligations than those of the single state. Mary stands ready to help all who seek her aid in making genuine commitments and living up to them. This is what her *fiat* meant in her own life. In our expressions of consent to God's will—our chosen commitments—we imitate her consent to be the Mother of the Redeemer.

Most of the titles given to the Blessed Virgin signify her perpetual role in heaven, from where she mediates Christ's graces to man. Some, however, also include her life on earth as a historic character and associate of her Son. These, particularly the titles that refer to her perpetual virginity, have both a heavenly and an earthly meaning. Of those titles and descriptive phrases derived from the Fathers, Pope Pius XII lists "Lily Among Thorns, Land

Wholly Intact, Immaculate, Free From All Contagion Of Sin," and many more.[9] The titles that the Church confers upon the Virgin describe her manner of life and indicate the distinct holiness with which she lived out her vocation.

Mary's vocation is, in short, to say *fiat* over and over again to God, from her girlhood through the present and throughout all the future of human life. In her fulfillment of this calling we see her as the foremost type of the Church and the universal Mother of the human race.

Because she was the first believer in her Son's divinity and the first devotee of his divine will, Mary became a type of the Church. This means that she is drawn from the Church, the Mystical Body of Christ, and that she is the preeminent exemplar of Church membership. Just as her role in salvation history makes her, like Christ, a mirror of the Scriptures, so she is a mirror of everything that a Christian should be. As such, she strongly embodies the model of holiness toward which every member of the Church should strive. In her cooperation with God's call, she "represented in some sort all human kind,"[10] all of whom are called to membership in the Church. She responded to the angel Gabriel's announcement not just for herself, but "in the name of the Church."[11] Furthermore, the Vicar of Christ proclaimed Mary "a model of the spiritual attitude with which the Church celebrates and lives the divine mysteries ... a most excellent exemplar of the Church in the order of faith, charity and perfect union with Christ."[12]

The same pope, Paul VI, gives us grounds for asserting that Mary's offering of Christ in the Temple is an exercise of the priestly

---

[9] *Ibid.*, no. 9.

[10] Pope Leo XIII, *Octobri Mense*, no. 4, citing St. Thomas Aquinas.

[11] Pope Paul VI, *Marialis Cultus*, no. 18.

[12] *Ibid.*, no. 16.

capacity given to all Christians, not through Holy Orders but through Baptism, which confers the common capacity to offer valid sacrifices in the name of our High Priest, Jesus Christ. The Church, writes the Holy Father, "has detected in the heart of the Virgin taking her Son to Jerusalem to present him to the Lord (cf. Luke 2:22) a desire to make an offering … that exceeds the ordinary meaning of the rite."[13] We may believe that Mary's offering of Jesus in accord with the law transcended the requirements of the law because of the supreme value of the Offering. But we, too, offer Jesus to the Father. We, too, offer "a more perfect sacrifice" than the blood of mere animals. Through the Son and in his name, we also can be made an "everlasting gift" to the Father.[14] When we become such a gift, we will be acting in imitation of Mary.

We should, however, always remember that it is the *mode* of Mary's exemplarity that makes her an example for all of us. The disposition of her heart is what does this—not the historic accidents of her life. Although in her origin and life she was perfectly holy, her vocation took the form of an obedience that is accessible to everyone in all ages. She is

> an example to be imitated, not precisely in the type of life she led, and much less for the socio-cultural background in which she lived and which today scarcely exists anywhere. She is held up as an example to the faithful rather for the way in which, in her own particular life, she fully and responsibly accepted the will of God (cf. Luke 1:38), because she heard the word of God and acted on it, and because charity and a spirit of service were the driving force of her actions.[15]

---

[13] *Ibid.*, no. 20.
[14] Eucharistic Prayer No. 3.
[15] Pope Paul VI, *Marialis Cultus*, no. 35.

For this reason, Mary's example extends to everyone. It reaches the "modern woman," for instance, who, in the midst of societal rebellion against not only God and the Church, but also against nature and biology, is still called to Mary's kind of vocation. For "Mary of Nazareth … was a woman who did not hesitate to proclaim that God vindicates the humble and the oppressed … a woman of strength, who experienced poverty and suffering, flight and exile."[16] Pope John Paul II has made the relevance of the Blessed Virgin to the condition and calling of the women of today a particular emphasis.[17]

It is precisely in her acceptance of the human condition—amplified as its suffering was through her unique calling—that she was preparing for an eternity of service to her children on earth. This is the last chapter of the Virgin's vocation. It will endure until the end of time. She accomplished all of her earthly task in preparation for this. For after her earthly service as the "handmaid of the Lord," which brought her a major role "in the laborious expiation made by her Son for the sins of the World," she entered his presence to remain eternally. There, "without measure and without end will she be able to plead our cause."[18]

This perpetual role of the Blessed Virgin—the apex of her vocation—is the focus of much of the Church's teaching about her. One great pope of the Rosary, Leo XIII, repeatedly mentioned Mary's enduring devotion to her salvific calling. It is, he taught, "her greatest pleasure to grant her help and comfort to those who seek her."[19] Mary had more immediate access to the Son and the

---

[16] Ibid., no. 37.

[17] See, for instance, Address to Women Religious, Turin, September 4, 1988 ("May the Mother of the Church be an inspiration for the discovery of a new feminine identity"), and Letter to Women (preparatory to the Beijing conference), June 29, 1995.

[18] Pope Leo XIII, Iucunda Semper Expectatione, September 8, 1894, nos. 3 and 4.

[19] Supremi Apostolatus Officio (Encyclical on the Devotion of the Rosary), September 1, 1883, no. 2.

"mercy and truth" that he created than any other human being. Now, "Mary is the intermediary through whom is distributed unto us this immense treasure of mercies gathered by God."[20] Mary is the one "to whom we may confess our designs and our actions, our innocence and our repentance, our torments and our joys, our prayers and our desires."[21] This is the role to which God called her and toward which her life was directed.

This continuing dedication to human well-being brings to mind the great St. Thérèse of Lisieux, whose determination to "spend [her] eternity saving souls" bears such a clear resemblance to Our Lady's ardent concern for mankind. Even today, as Pope Pius XII taught, Mary "repeats to each of us those words with which she addressed the servers at the wedding feast of Cana, pointing … to Jesus Christ, 'Whatsoever he shall say to you, do ye.'"[22] Mary, Pope Paul VI stated, "continues to be spiritually present to all her redeemed children, being constantly inspired in this noble function by the Uncreated Love which is the soul of the Mystical Body and its ultimate source of life."[23]

"*This noble function*": fulfilling a vocation is always an action, whether spiritual or physical. The Blessed Virgin's undying activity on our behalf is a continued response to God's call, a continued *fiat*.

It is small wonder that so many phrases and titles that the Church applies to Mary refer to this heavenly activity. She is the "minister to us of heavenly grace,"[24] "an intercessor mighty in fa-

---

[20] *Octobri Mense*, no. 4.

[21] *Ibid.*, no. 5.

[22] *Fulgens Corona*, no. 25, referring to John 2:5.

[23] *The Holy Spirit and Mary* (Letter of Pope Paul VI to Cardinal Léon Josef von Suenens on the Occasion of the International Marian Congress), May 13, 1975.

[24] Pope Leo XIII, *Supremi Apostolatus Officio*, no. 1.

vor with God,"[25] "the seat of all divine graces ... adorned with all gifts of the Holy Spirit, ... Reparatrix of the first parents, the giver of life to posterity."[26] She reigns as Queen in heaven, but her royalty has done nothing to diminish her zeal for helping her weak and sinful children. On the contrary. Just as Jesus' eternal kingship is manifest in service and sacrifice, Mary's reign is wholly devoted to his interests.

These interests lead to a final aspect of Mary's vocation—her role as Mother of Christians and of the human race. I have discussed how the Blessed Virgin is a type of the Church. She is the first and best disciple of Christ, the concentration of all Christian virtues. But, as the Mother of Christ—the Mother of God, the Theotokos—she is also the Mother of the Church. Pope St. Pius X writes of her maternal role:

> Mary, carrying the Savior within her, may be said to have also carried all those whose life was contained in the life of the Savior. Therefore all of us who are united to Christ ... have issued from the womb of Mary like a body united to its head. Hence, though in a spiritual and mystical fashion, we are all children of Mary, and she is Mother of us all.[27]

The motherhood of Mary is made explicit at the Crucifixion, where Jesus designated St. John the son of the Virgin. *Our* filial relationship to the Mother of God comes in part from our fraternal relationship with St. John.

Moreover, because God graciously condescended to fraternity with the human race, all human beings bear a filial relation-

---

[25] Pope Leo XIII, *Octobri Mense*, no. 4.

[26] Pope Pius IX, *Ineffabilis Deus*.

[27] *Ad Diem Illum Laetissimum* (Encyclical on the Immaculate Conception), February 2, 1904, no. 10.

ship to his Mother. We are all her children. St. Irenaeus, in a frequently quoted passage, states that Mary "has been constituted the cause of salvation for the whole human race."[28] Her maternal relationship to mankind depends upon her role in salvation history as the Mother of our Lord.

Mary's universal motherhood comprises a natural and supernatural life focused on her Son in at least three ways. It is, first, the loving response of a God-fearing mother to her child. This is the starting point for most meditations on Mary's maternity, and for most works of art that depict the Madonna and Child. These images are reflections of a true archetype, Mother and Baby, that was implanted by experience in the human psyche before *Homo sapiens* learned to speak.

Second, Mary's mind is completely centered on *obedience* to God's will—which in her case is the will of Jesus. This striking contrast to the ordinary human situation, in which the child obeys the mother, is a natural result of the identity of this specific Son. That identity, in turn—the true form that God's great condescension took—is underscored by the fact that her Son and Creator was in turn obedient to *her*, that he "learned obedience" to his Father "through what he suffered" (Hebrews 5:8), that he "humbled himself and became obedient even unto death" (Philippians 2:8)— that, in short, his entire mission was a form of subordination to a fallen race and to its only unfallen member, his Mother. The instruction "Do whatever he tells you" (John 2:5) is Mary's last recorded utterance. We are invited—indeed required—to apply these words to ourselves. It is clear that Mary applied them to herself profoundly. In true maternal fashion she wishes all that is really best for those her Son came to save—that is, for all mankind. "Do

---

[28] *Against Heresies*. Quoted in several papal documents, among them Pope Pius XII, *Ingruentium Malorum* (Encyclical on Reciting the Rosary), September 15, 1951, no. 6.

whatever he tells you" is the principle of her vocation. In the fulfillment of her own mission, this demanding rule led to a "community of will and suffering between Christ and Mary."[29] For to be the Mother of her Son meant to suffer as he suffered. Mary was the first to learn the "cost of discipleship." To be the Mother of this particular Son, to whom she owed obedience of heart and act, was also to accept all whom he named brothers and sisters as her own children. Such conformity to the divine will made the Blessed Virgin both the type of Christians and the Mother of those whom he designated coheirs of the Kingdom, which is open to all human beings.

My third observation regarding the Virgin's Christ-centered maternity is this: Mary's emotional and physical care for her divine Son is, by the logic of his own words, care for the entire human race. Like any dutiful mother, Mary consoled her Son when he was a child. She also dressed, fed, and housed him. She undoubtedly identified with his suffering on a thousand unrecorded instances, completing it by her empathy and being further sanctified by it—if that which is already completely holy can be further sanctified. Later, however, in his profound identification with the suffering and downtrodden of the human race, Jesus taught that he is himself the recipient of our works of mercy:

> Then the righteous will answer him saying, "Lord, when did we see you hungry and feed you, or thirsty and give you to drink? And when did we see you a stranger and take you in, or naked and clothe you?" And in answer the King will say to them, "Amen, I say to you, insofar as you did it for one of these least of my brothers, you did it for me" (Matthew 25:37-40; SPCE).

---

[29] Pope Pius X, *Ad Diem Illum Laetissimum*, no. 12.

16

By a simple substitution, we can see that Mary's care for Christ implies care for all with whom he identifies. Her maternal care extends to everyone.

All our acts of charity toward the needy align us with Mary's care for her Son. We resemble her in caring for Christ—visiting, consoling, feeding, clothing, housing, counseling him—as he comes to us poor and poor in spirit, injured and mourning. Inasmuch as I care for Christ's least brothers, I honor and resemble Mary.

And that brings me to a final observation about the Blessed Virgin's vocation. All of the Church's teaching about the Mother of God points to the fact that we are called to a vocation that essentially resembles hers. She is a type of the Church. She is a model Christian. She was the first and most faithful believer in Christ. Her life was totally conformed to his. We are called to strive toward all of this in the conduct of our lives. Furthermore, if by the grace of God we succeed, our end will resemble hers. As a result of her faithfulness—and of the filial duty Jesus owed her—she was exalted at the time of her passage from this world, often referred to as her dormition; she was not allowed to "see corruption," forever free of the consequences of death that he had conquered and delivered her from. In heaven, eternally in his presence, she continues to listen with motherly care to the cries of her children.

In our small way, we are called to the same glory. Mary's triumph heralds our own. As Jesus was "raised from the dead, the first fruits of those who have fallen asleep" (1 Corinthians 15:20), he extended his victory to his first follower, whom he honors both as Mother and disciple. If we respond to God's call to us to "do whatever he tells you," we will be like Mary in the fulfillment of our own vocations. And when we finally triumph over death because of him, Jesus will similarly call us, his innumerable lesser followers, to share in the vision of God's face forever.

(b) The Gateway

The school of Christian virtue. The Church has often emphasized the use of the Rosary as an important part of one's spiritual and prayer life. One of the theses of this book is that the Rosary can provide a framework for much of one's daily meditation. It can be our *customary* gateway by which to draw near to Christ. It is a means of "praying without ceasing" (cf. 1 Thessalonians 5:17) —which means, not that one never lapses from direct discourse with God, or still less that one's prayers are interminably verbose, but that one doesn't stop returning habitually to the Lord for guidance, strength, and forgiveness. The Rosary is "that devotion which our ancestors were in the habit of practicing, not only as an ever-ready remedy for their misfortunes, but as a whole badge of Christian piety."[30] Note that the Rosary is only one such badge. The others include the Divine Office and weekly or even daily attendance at the Sacrifice of the Mass. Nothing can substitute for the Mass. But as an entrance and pathway for one's daily private prayer the Rosary is unmatched.

This is true, first, because the other thesis of this book is true: the mysteries of the Rosary are a mirror of Scripture. The Holy Father wrote in 1892, "[T]he Rosary offers an easy way to present the chief mysteries of the Christian religion and to impress them upon the mind."[31] These mysteries are nothing but the heart of the New Testament, which resounds with echoes of the entire Bible.

As Christians and Catholics we should pray constantly for our own conversion. We should beseech God that our prayers and worship may not be mere wind, but that they will produce a real change in our lives—that they will bring us to "transformation in

---

[30] Pope Leo XIII, *Supremi Apostolatus Officio*, no. 10.

[31] Pope Leo XIII, *Magnae Dei Matris* (Encyclical on the Rosary), September 8, 1892, no. 14.

Christ," Dietrich von Hildebrand's phrase that denotes Christian growth in the likeness of Jesus. This transformation is, of course, the Lord's work and not our own, but we must strive daily to make ourselves receptive to it. The Rosary is one of the best devotions for this purpose. It is

> a stimulus and spur to the practice of evangelic virtues which it injects and cultivates in our souls. Above all, it nourishes the Catholic Faith, which flourishes again by due meditation on the sacred mysteries, and raises minds to the truth revealed to us by God.[32]

Of great importance is the fact that in this time of family collapse—when the very meaning of "family" is under attack from anti-Christian ideologies—the Rosary nourishes not only the individual's faith, but the faith and unity of the family. As Pope Paul VI teaches, the Second Vatican Council's emphasis on the family as a "domestic Church" is invaluable to an understanding of the true mission of the family. The family is the chief context of education in faith and morals, in the social graces, in forgiveness and mutual support. And the "family Rosary" is a vital part of life in this "domestic sanctuary." As we see family life disintegrating around us, we must make a "concrete effort to reinstate communal prayer" in our own families "if there is to be a restoration of the theological concept of the family as the domestic Church."[33] Making such an effort will help families to "live in full measure [their] vocation and spirituality."[34] Because the family is the basic social unit, healing families is essential to healing our society. Who can doubt that what occurs in the heart of families indicates what

---

[32] Pope Pius XI, *Ingravescentibus Malis*, no. 22.

[33] *Marialis Cultus*, no. 52.

[34] *Ibid.*, no. 54.

family members will do outside the home? If the Rosary were a gateway to nothing besides healthy family spirituality, it would still be worth all the effort we could give it. But as it is, the Rosary can "form the most efficacious school of Christian discipline and Christian virtue."[35]

Furthermore, the Rosary is a gateway open to all. That is the reason it has always been known as a "popular" devotion—a devotion of the *populus*, the people. It presents the great chapters of salvation history "to every kind of mind, however unskilled," and proposes them "less as truths or doctrines to be speculated upon than as present facts to be seen and perceived."[36] In the Rosary the truth of the Gospel is not questioned, as it often is questioned in the critiques of scholars. Because those who practice the devotion of the Rosary receive the mysteries as the word of God, this prayer can represent the greatest treasure of God's riches, which are revealed to receptive minds but often hidden from critical ones.

A *powerful means of supplication*. The use of the Rosary as a prayer for specific intentions has grown through the centuries. That is perhaps the most important "gateway" feature of this great devotion. Specifically, a main theme of this book is that the spiritual meanings of the mysteries make each of them particularly suitable for one's individual intentions. The gateway is internal to the mysteries and related to their subject matter. It opens upon all the variety of the human scene. The applications of the Joyful Mysteries to family life and to the pro-life movement, for instance, make these biblical scenes perfect meditations for petitions about one's own children and about some of the most distressing current social evils. That is why this book recommends intentions for each

---

[35] Pope Pius XII, *Ingruentium Malorum*, no. 14.

[36] Pope Leo XIII, *Iucunda Semper Expectatione*, no. 8. Cf. Pope Pius XII, *Ingruentium Malorum*, no. 8.

mystery: they are suggested by the mystery itself, though sometimes rather loosely; and they have grown organically with my own use of the Rosary as a framework for prayers about the world in which I live.

In its origin and development the Rosary was offered not only as a prayer of praise, and not only for the intentions expressed in the words of the *Our Father* and the *Hail Mary*, but for needs specific to the times. The common Western form of the Rosary is traditionally said to have been given to St. Dominic, and the Dominicans were for centuries particularly associated with it. Tradition holds that the Rosary was instrumental in the defeat of the Albigensian heresy in the thirteenth century. As a historical fact, the defeat of the Turkish Muslim forces at Lepanto on October 7, 1571, led Pope St. Pius V to institute the memorial of Our Lady of the Rosary, for he attributed the Christian victory to Mary. Throughout the more recent history of the Rosary, the offering of its prayers for definite intentions has been encouraged more and more by the Magisterium. Like his saintly predecessor, Pope Leo XIII attributed the Christian victory at Lepanto over the threat of "superstition and barbarism" to Our Lady of Victories.[37] On many occasions he and other Vicars of Christ have noted that the Rosary is especially suited "to obviate impending dangers" and combat "pernicious heresiarchs and heresies."[38] As a weapon against threats to the Church, according to the Holy Father, the Rosary is a potent weapon, whether these threats take the form of "insults and outrages against our August religion"[39] or the "dangerous phenomenon of recourse to arms," which brings about "unspeakable sufferings."[40]

---

[37] *Supremi Apostolatus Officio*, no. 4.

[38] *Ibid.*, no. 5, citing Pope Sixtus IV and Pope Leo X.

[39] Pope Leo XIII, *Iucunda Semper Expectatione*, no. 9

[40] Pope Paul VI, *Mense Maio*, April 30, 1965.

On the positive side, reflection on the mysteries of the Rosary brings us "lessons ... for the leading of an honest life" based on "that earthly and divine home of holiness, the House of Nazareth," the "all-perfect model of domestic society."[41] It is the positive uses of the Rosary that I want especially to encourage by this book. For every evil that besets us there is a corresponding blessing. Every pain that we suffer can, if endured in union with Christ and his holy Mother, increase our own holiness. When we meditate on the mysteries and seek to understand the analogies between them and our own situation, all of our concerns can be translated into meaningful, Gospel-based offerings to God. The Rosary can become an effective prayer on behalf of the people we meet daily, on behalf of the loved ones from whom we are estranged, and on behalf of everyone to whom our lives and prayers pertain. (Try this: if you pray the Rosary while going about your daily affairs, offer the petition "Pray for us sinners now and at the hour of our death" for everyone within your field of vision and immediate consciousness. You will find your charity increasing as you become more of an intercessor for others.) At the same time, our ability to embody the virtues exemplified in the mysteries will be greatly enhanced. The Rosary will become an ever more eloquent invitation to Jesus Christ to transform our lives and the lives of those around us. Thus will we make our own the vocation of Our Lady, who was wholly transformed by her Son.

That vocation, I repeat, is devotedly centered on God. So are the mysteries of the Rosary. Mary's worshipful gaze is always directed toward Jesus. Toward him she directs us. With the Holy Spirit as her strength, she bids us observe the teaching and example of Christ and "do whatever he tells" us. She would abhor any near-

---

[41] Pope Leo XIII, *Laetitiae Sanctae* (On the Rosary), September 8, 1893, no. 6.

sighted devotion that failed to focus on Christ. For "the ultimate purpose of devotion to the Blessed Virgin is to glorify God and to lead Christians to commit themselves to a life which is in absolute conformity with His will."[42] God grant such grace to every reader of this book.

---

[42] Pope Paul VI, *Marialis Cultus*, no. 39.

Chapter Two

THE JOYFUL MYSTERIES

"The 'fullness of time' denotes 'the moment
when the Holy Spirit, who had already infused the
fullness of grace into Mary of Nazareth, formed in her
virginal womb the human nature of Christ.'
This 'fullness' marks the moment when, with the
entrance of the eternal into time, time itself is
redeemed, and being filled with the mystery of Christ
becomes definitively 'salvation time.'"

Pope John Paul II

1

THE ANNUNCIATION

Littera: Scripture and gloss. The scriptural account of the Annunciation is found in Luke 1:26-38:

> Now in the sixth month the angel Gabriel was sent from God to a city of Galilee named Nazareth, to a virgin who was betrothed to a man of the house of David named Joseph; and the virgin's name was Mary. And when he came into her presence he said, "Hail, full of grace, the Lord is with you!" She was greatly perplexed by this saying, and wondered what sort of greeting this might be. Then the angel said to her, "Fear not, Mary, for you have found favor with God. And behold, you will conceive in your womb and will bear a son, and you shall name him Jesus. He will be great, and will be called the Son of the Most High; and the Lord God will give him the throne of his father, David. He will reign over the house of Jacob for ever, and his kingdom will have no end." And Mary said to the angel, "How will this come about, since I do not know man?" And the angel said to her, "The Holy Spirit will come upon you, and the power of the Most High will overshadow you; therefore the holy child to be born will be called the Son of God. And behold, your kinswoman Elizabeth, even in her old age, has conceived a son; and this is the sixth month with her who was called barren. For nothing will be impossible for God." And Mary said, "Behold, I am the handmaid of the Lord; let it be done to me according to your word." Then the angel went away from her.

At its simplest, this is an account of a virgin named Mary who is visited by an angel named Gabriel. The girl is undoubtedly at prayer, as her encounter with the supernatural would suggest. She is certainly alone. When the angel appears to her, he greets her with a salutation, part of which is later incorporated into the prayer *Hail Mary*. But his words are mysterious, and Mary finds them very troubling. The angel senses her apprehension and tells her not to fear, since she has "found favor with God." As a result of that favor, Gabriel says that she is to "conceive in [her] womb and will bear a son," who is to be named Jesus. This Jesus, the heavenly messenger asserts, is the Son of God (the "Most High") and the Son of David. His reign over the "house of Jacob" will never end.

Mary, however, is not so sure, and the angel's waiting for her response makes clear that Mary's consent is needed: she is being *asked* to cooperate with God, not commanded to do so. She has had no sexual relations and therefore cannot imagine becoming pregnant. The angel tells her that Jesus is to be engendered by the Holy Spirit—that is, by God, the "Most High"—and that "the holy child to be born" will consequently "be called the Son of God." To help Mary believe the message, the angel announces that Elizabeth, Mary's cousin, previously considered sterile, is now six months pregnant. Elizabeth's pregnancy, it is implied, has been wrought by God, for whom "nothing will be impossible." Mary declares herself the maidservant of the Lord and expresses her consent to whatever God wants of her. Then the angel leaves.

Further context. The Annunciation is infinitely rich in meaning and is worth a lifetime's prayerful meditation. One could never exhaust its profounder meanings, many of which are at the heart of the Christian faith revealed in Scripture and handed down in the Church by the successors of the apostles. For this passage of Scripture records the historic moment of the Incarnation of God and embodies many of its most important features.

First, the divinity of the child is repeatedly and clearly affirmed. This is the story of the very instant at which God Almighty charges into his own creation,[1] where he is eventually to be ridiculed and killed. Though at the time of the Annunciation the third person of the Blessed Trinity had not been clearly revealed, the writer, working after Jesus had left the earth, had an understanding of the Holy Spirit, who had been given to the followers of Christ at Pentecost. By the inspiration of the Holy Spirit the sacred writer sees in retrospect the working of the same Spirit at the Annunciation. It is the Holy Spirit and the "power of the Most High," Saint Luke affirms, who "will overshadow" the Virgin. The evangelist twice declares that the child is to be the Son of God. The term "Most High," though a descriptive phrase and not a personal name, is a standard name of the Creator in Jewish tradition.[2] By affirming that the child to be born is the "Son of God" and the "Son of the Most High," Saint Luke unambiguously declares that the Creator whom the chosen people have worshiped since the time of Abraham is the child's Father. God thus breaks into nature—as man narrowly conceives nature—in order directly to cause the birth of Christ, an event that was both supernatural and natural in the highest sense; for with relation to the Creator of all that is, the distinction between nature and supernature is

---

[1] My use of the word *charge* comes from the frontispiece of Robert Frost's *In the Clearing* (New York: Holt, Rinehart, and Winston, 1962): "But God's own descent/ Into flesh was meant/ As a demonstration/ That the supreme merit/ Lay in risking spirit/ In substantiation./ Spirit enters flesh/ And for all it's worth/ Charges into earth/ In birth after birth/ Ever fresh and fresh./ We may take the view/ That its derring-do/ Thought of in the large/ Is one mighty charge/ On our human part/ Of the soul's ethereal/ Into the material." The image is apt. I don't think Frost intended to suggest a belief in reincarnation.

[2] Cf. Deuteronomy 32:8: "When the Most High gave to the nations their inheritance ... he fixed the bounds of the peoples according to the number of the sons of God," and Acts 7:48: "the Most High does not dwell in houses made with hands."

nonexistent.[3] It is the nature of God, who sustains all of creation, to be able to suspend its laws.

Second, Jesus, the child to be born, is the fulfillment of the covenant that God first made with Abraham and subsequently reiterated throughout the history of Abraham's family. In that pact, sealed with the sign of circumcision, God promised Abraham a multitude of descendants and a desirable homeland, "the land of Canaan, for an everlasting possession" (Genesis 17:8). The Lord further promised that in Abraham's offspring "all the families of the earth shall be blessed" (Genesis 12:3[4]). Throughout the history of the Jewish nation, which took the name of Abraham's grandson Israel (formerly Jacob), God continues to restate his promise and to fulfill it faithfully. His people, however, waver from their part of the covenant by continuing to fall into idolatry of one sort or another, from which they must be recalled by exile, slavery, plagues, or other punishment. God's chosen people believe, at least intermittently, in his promise, and they keep faith, at least sometimes, with him.

But over the ages they see that their understanding of God's justice does not accord well with the evidence. The book of Job, for instance, teaches them that rewards do not seem to be distributed according to merit in this world. Job suffers for no apparent serious reason, although he is true to God. Peace is fleeting or illusory even in the Promised Land, where all too often positions of worldly honor are held by men who strut and flaunt their indifference toward God and oppress his people. "Where is God?" his people ask, "and why does he not act to bring justice?" Again and

---

[3]   See C.S. Lewis, *Miracles* (New York: Macmillan, 1947). Lewis's analysis of miracles, of "how God intervenes in nature and human affairs," is a masterpiece of Christian apologetic. See also his discussion of the words *nature* and *natural* in *Studies in Words* (2nd. ed., Cambridge: Cambridge University Press, 1967).

[4]   Alternate reading: "by you [Abraham] all the families of the earth shall bless themselves."

again the Psalms invoke God's help against the injustice that often persists regardless of the afflicted ones' service and devotion to him. In Psalm 74, for instance, the speaker cries out, "O God, why dost thou cast us off for ever?" and laments that "the enemy scoffs, and an impious people reviles thy name." He concludes with a plea to God: "remember the clamor of thy foes, the uproar of thy adversaries which goes up continually." Psalm 44 and 73 contain similar elements; so do all of the psalms that prefigure the Messiah's suffering, such as the great Psalm 22.

In this situation a Savior is needed, someone who will bring the promised rewards to God's servants. And the Israelites looked forward to his advent: "Oh, that deliverance for Israel would come out of Zion! When the Lord restores the fortunes of his people, Jacob shall rejoice and Israel shall be glad" (Psalm 14:7). The psalmist looks forward, in other words, to the messianic restoration of Israel, which will fulfill the ancient covenant. But according to Saint Paul—and to the great surprise and disappointment of many in Israel—the lowly Jesus of Nazareth is that "offspring" of Abraham that God promised in the covenant (Galatians 3:16).

The paragon of earthly kings, David, foreshadows the reign of his descendant. But whereas David's proper reign had ended centuries before, the Gospel tells us that the Son to be born of Mary will reign "without end." Clearly, the reign is a supernatural one and not just that of a powerful earthly king who will assert the rights of Israel against Rome and other overlords. The latter is undoubtedly the kind of reign that the Jewish people generally expected, and their disappointment at the Messiah who actually came caused them to reject him. But surely this is the heart of the Israelites' sacred tradition: that the coming reign of the Messiah is a spiritual and not an earthly kingdom.[5] The new ruler over the "house

---

[5] The Israelites rejected the Messiah because they had a false idea of what he would be like. Similarly, "liberation theology" rejects the Messiah who really exists by claiming

of Jacob" is to reconstitute that house so that it will include "all nations." The new king is to fulfill in literal fact the prophetic blessing invoked upon David in hyperbole: "May he live while the sun endures, and as long as the moon, throughout all generations" (Psalm 72:5). The eternal reign of Christ is clearly here foreshadowed. It is explicitly stressed in the New Testament. On the solemnity of Christ the King, the Office of Readings quotes the Lord in the book of Revelation: "Fear not, I am the First and the Last and the living one; I died, and behold I am alive for evermore, and I have the keys of Death and Hades" (Revelation 1:17-18). The birth of *this* Son of David brings heaven and earth together. It presages his eternal rule after time and perishable creation are left behind. Advent and apocalypse are therefore joined in the Annunciation.

And then there is Mary. He who is to fulfill the covenant is the Son of God. But, without diminishing the centrality of Christ to the plan of salvation, one can see that the account of the Annunciation is as much about the Mother of God as her Son. Though what is said about her serves to focus our eyes on the Lord himself—as all the mysteries do—this Gospel passage says much about the Blessed Mother. In it Saint Luke insists upon two points about her: that she is a virgin, and that she submissively—indeed joyfully—cooperates in bringing the Son into the world.

First, the evangelist is at pains to teach emphatically that Mary is a virgin. She is twice called a virgin. Then she affirms her virginity herself by stating that she has not "known man"—i.e.,

---

that Jesus' mission was mainly an earthly one. In doing so this theology explicitly rejects the words of the Savior himself: "My kingship is not of this world" (John 18:36). The actual reign of Christ therefore satisfies neither those who, like the Israelites, want a peaceful earthly theocracy nor those who, like the liberationists, want a utopian commune.

that she has had no conjugal relations.[6] Further, the affirmation that the child is "Son of God" and "Son of the Most High" means precisely that he is *not* the son of a man (though it also, of course, means much more than that). Hence he is necessarily the son of a virgin, and Mary's "fruitful virginity"[7] is again affirmed. The inspired text therefore certainly affirms that the Lord's beginning as a man is miraculous, the result of a union between God and a virgin. Jesus takes his full humanity from his Mother. In addition to her cooperation, this means that she contributes the ovum that is fertilized to form his body. Otherwise, she wouldn't truly be his Mother. In our technologically advanced but spiritually retarded culture we call a woman in whom somebody else's fertilized egg is implanted a "surrogate mother." But Mary is no surrogate; she is the real thing, and from her comes the complete mother's portion of the genetic material that shapes Jesus the man.

In Saint Luke's second main point about Mary, her cooperation with God, we see her move quickly through a range of fearful emotions to an expression of acceptance. The latter is the result of a rational decision. She is afraid at first—greatly "perplexed" at the strangeness of the heavenly visitor and his greeting. Fear at a direct confrontation with the supernatural is normal. Moses, for instance, at the theophany of the burning bush, "hid his face, for he was afraid to look at God" (Exodus 3:6). Mary is also confused: the meaning of the angel's greeting, being so far removed from all previous human experience, is not at all clear to her. As she later ponders the actions and words of her twelve-year-old Son in the Temple, so she ponders the words of the angel here. She is subject

---

[6] I once heard a learned Catholic man say that Mary probably didn't know what made babies anyway. He clearly had not read the Gospel with any attention.

[7] Pope Paul VI, *Marialis Cultus*, February 2, 1974, no. 11.

to sudden fear like all of us. But it is important to understand that her purity of mind and her devotion to the will of God are *not* emotions, but habitual acts of will. By her will she rises above her fear in this short scene and, with a self-discipline formed through habitual choosing of God's will in preference to other considerations, joins his will to hers in perfect harmony: *Fiat mihi secundum verbum tuum*—"Be it done to me according to thy word." In calling herself the maidservant of the Lord and acquiescing wholly in his will, she foreshadows the adult will of her divine Son, whose only desire is to do what the Father wills. By her acceptance of her profound vocation she also becomes the prototypical Christian, the first and greatest model, after the Lord himself, for Christians to emulate.

Extensions and applications. How should we respond to the Annunciation? What is its meaning for our time? The verses of the *Angelus* offer a key:

1. "The angel of the Lord declared unto Mary, and she conceived by the Holy Spirit."
2. [Mary answers,] "Behold the handmaid of the Lord; be it done to me according to thy word."
3. [The conclusion:] "And the Word became flesh and dwelt among us."

Our first response—indeed, the first response of anyone in any era—should be gratitude for the Incarnation. As Jesus was "begotten of the Father before all worlds," so he became a man on our fallen planet, and his presence among us perdures. When we think our lives are too complicated, when we think the attraction of sin is too compelling, when we are tempted to despair of our own salvation and that of the people we love, we should remember gratefully that God, who cannot lie, came to live among us as a man and promised to remain with us always. By becoming a part of things, the Creator of all things guaranteed that all will be made new. His Spirit enlivens the world and moves it toward its heavenly regeneration. All attributes of nature are the object of his concern: "When you send forth your Spirit, they are created; and you renew the face of the earth" (Psalm 104:30, NAB). The Lord remains with us, as simple and insistent as a sanctuary candle beside the Blessed Sacrament, as homey and dependable as the Host whose bread-like appearance veils his true body. We should pray and strive never to forget that our Creator condescended to live in his own creation in order to redeem his servants from sin and death. This is what was announced by the Annunciation.

Our gratitude for the Incarnation, however, also belongs to Mary. When we express our thanks to God for his bounty—as we should, regularly and persistently—we should also thank the angels and saints, who, in their goodness, love and pray for us. Their freely chosen concern for our welfare, which springs from their love of God, leads such saints as St. Thérèse of Lisieux to busy themselves praying for us constantly. But if we thank the departed holy ones in the Communion of Saints, how much greater should be our gratitude to Mary, the Queen of Saints? Because of her our Creator became our brother, our neighbor (as in the parable of the Good Samaritan, Luke 10:25-37), our fellow man. Because Mary cooperated with the Holy Spirit, God himself took on the whole human condition, including subjectivity to death, so that he might show us the way to resurrection and eternal life. Because of her submission to the will of God, Mary is called by the traditional name Foederis Arca, the Ark of the Covenant, for she bears into the world the Savior who is the fulfillment of God's ancient promise. Just as the signs of the ancient covenant, such as the tables of stone on which the Ten Commandments were written, were borne in a gold-covered ark of acacia wood, so Jesus, the fulfillment of the ancient covenant and the sacrament of the new covenant, was borne into the world in Mary's womb. Likewise, Mary became in a sense the original ciborium and chalice, for she bore God's body and blood into the world. Finally, because of her acquiescence in God's desire as expressed by the archangel Gabriel, Mary became *our* Mother, even before the confirmation of her "spiritual maternity" on Calvary.[8] We should be as grateful to Mary, our Mother, as was the child Jesus, our Brother. At the same time, we should pay honor where it is due: we should always remember that Jesus is no ordinary brother but God Almighty, and that Mary is our Queen as well as our Mother, honored by God himself above all other creatures.

A further and inescapable meaning of the Annunciation comes from the fact that when Mary agreed to Gabriel's announcement and the Lord was conceived in her uterus, he was *at that moment* the Incarnate Word. There was no time lag—indeed there can be none—between conception and "ensoulment," for the soul determines human existence from the beginning. What Mary conceived in her womb while the angel's breath still lingered in the room was a fully human being, not a "blob of tissue" or a devalued "product of conception," or a "potential person." The same is true of every other human being who has ever lived: we are all fully human from the moment of our conception.

---

[8] Mary is "a Mother to us in the order of grace" because of her role in the plan of salvation. She was prepared by God to bear his Son into the world, she shared in his life, death, and resurrection, and in heaven she still "cares for the brethren of her Son", *Lumen Gentium* ([*Dogmatic Constitution on the Church*], in *Vatican Council II: The Conciliar and Post Conciliar Documents*, ed. Austin Flannery [Study Edition, Northport, New York: Costello, 1987]), nos. 61-62. The scene at Calvary in which Jesus commends Mary and St. John to each other as Mother and son cements the Blessed Virgin's maternal role in the Church and world. For an excellent article on Mary's role as Mother of all human beings, see Arthur B. Calkins, "Mary's Spiritual Maternity," *Homiletic and Pastoral Review*, January 1996, pp. 7-17. Calkins not only takes the Infancy Narrative seriously, as the Church always has, but supplies a brief and trenchant critique of modernists who devalue Scripture. Then he presents a wide-ranging summary of patristic and magisterial teaching on the spiritual motherhood of the Blessed Virgin.

And that leads naturally to a current cultural application. St. Thomas Aquinas follows Aristotle in teaching that the soul is the substantial form of the body—that is, that the soul gives the body (and mind) its shape and its powers.[9] Only a human soul can start a human body in its development. No matter how small a human body is, it can never develop into a radish or a cat or a turtle or anything nonhuman, for a human body is actuated by a *human* soul from the moment of its conception. The acceptance of abortion has been based in part on the lie that an unborn child is not human "in the fullest sense." This claim has helped rationalize the taking of millions and millions of innocent lives. But an overtly false position can be maintained only for so long. New signs are popping up here and there that offer some hope that the tide may be changing. Some abortion advocates now admit the full humanity of the unborn child but think that there are reasons which would justify the taking of their lives. Thus Satan continues to deceive humankind by asserting that unspeakable evil can be legitimately chosen—or, rather, that it is not evil at all. The simple denial of moral truth has, of course, gone on since the beginning; Satan said to Eve, "You will not die" but "will be like God" (Genesis 3:4,5). But we have gone further. As we approach irrefutable clarity on what abortion is really about, a reality that has always been barely hidden by the pretensions of pro-abortion forces, we should remember that Jesus became human *at conception*: at the words of the angel, "The Word became flesh and dwelt among us," body and soul, humanity and divinity. Our choice as Christians is clear. Pope John Paul II has written with his usual courage, "*I confirm that the direct and voluntary killing of an innocent human being is always gravely*

---

[9] From the *Summa Theologiae* of St. Thomas Aquinas, 1a.75.5: The "very conception of soul … demands that it be a formative principle of some body." From 1a.75.1: "A soul, as the primary principle of life, is not a body but that which actuates a body."

immoral," and, "*I declare that direct abortion, abortion willed as an end or as a means, always constitutes a grave moral disorder, since it is the deliberate killing of an innocent human being.*"[10] "Choice" is really not valid here, except in the sense that we are capable of choosing unspeakable evil.

Finally, we must remember that Mary's *fiat* is related to our own. When we express our consent to God's will, especially in the decisive moments of life, we choose our own vocations. To fulfill them—to live up to our consent—often becomes our lifelong duty.

The Annunciation and the joy of Mary. In the Joyful Mysteries, Mary is very much a part of the story, whereas in the Sorrowful Mysteries she appears only briefly (on the Way of the Cross and at the Crucifixion). Her role in the first three of the Glorious Mysteries is muted, except as her glory is derived from her motherhood of Jesus. Then, at the end of the Rosary, with the Assumption and Coronation she becomes once again the central figure in the story, though even there she is the *object* of divine action and not the principal acting subject. Jesus, one way or another, is the main subject of all the mysteries.

Next to the astonishing news of the Incarnation itself, Mary's joy at accepting the will of God is the principal subject of the Annunciation. In this mystery she is therefore the principal human character, as depicted in numerous great works of art. We empathize with this holy Jewish girl and share her joy at bringing into the world the greatest possible gift to the whole human race.

Suggested intentions. The Blessed Virgin rejoiced to accept God's plan for her life. We should pray to do the same, in imitation of her and of her Son. This is our vocation. Also, because her

---

[10] *Evangelium Vitae* (*Origins*, 24.42 [April 6, 1995]), nos. 57 and 62; italics in original.

pregnancy is a great joy to her, Mary of the Annunciation embodies the proper attitude toward the gift of children. Accordingly, I have always offered this decade of the Rosary for my own children, for a list of other children for whom I want to pray (many of whom are no longer children), and for the needs of the children of the world. We should all pray for the Church of the future—that the children of the world will grow strong in the knowledge of Christ.

2

THE VISITATION

Littera: Scripture and gloss. Like the Annunciation, the story of the Visitation is recorded by St. Luke (1:39-56):

> Now in those days Mary set out and went with solicitude into the hill country to a city of Judah, and when she came into the house of Zechariah she greeted Elizabeth. And it happened that when Elizabeth heard Mary's greeting, the baby leaped in her womb and Elizabeth was filled with the Holy Spirit; and she exclaimed with a loud cry, "Blessed are you among women, and blessed is the fruit of your womb! And how is it that the mother of my Lord should come to *me*? For behold, when the sound of your greeting came to my ears, the baby in my womb leapt with a great joy. Blessed is she who believed that there would be a fulfillment of what was spoken to her by the Lord."

And Mary said,

"My soul magnifies the Lord,
and my spirit rejoices in God my Savior,
because he had regard for the lowliness of his handmaid.
For behold, henceforth all generations
shall call me blessed;
for the Mighty One has done great things for me,
and holy is his name.
And his mercy is from generation to generation
toward those who fear him.
He has shown might with his arm,

he has scattered the arrogant
in the conceit of their hearts,
he has pulled down the mighty from their thrones,
and exalted the lowly;
the hungry he has filled with good things,
and the rich he has sent empty away.
He has come to the aid of his servant, Israel,
mindful of his mercy,
just as he promised our fathers,
Abraham and his descendants forever."
Mary remained with her three months, and then
returned to her home.

In the Annunciation the archangel Gabriel announces *two* pregnancies, those of Mary and her kinswoman Elizabeth, whom we meet in person in the Visitation. Elizabeth's pregnancy, it is suggested, is a result of God's healing her barrenness. As a fore-runner of Elizabeth one thinks of Abraham's wife, Sarah, who was barren until she was old and then conceived Isaac with the help of God—but naturally, through sexual intercourse with Abraham (Genesis 21:1-7). The Old Testament contains no *specific* type for Mary's pregnancy, however, for it was brought about by the immediate and unprecedented action of God and not through a secondary cause such as Abraham. No ordinary human sperm was involved in the conception of Jesus; the Lord brought that pregnancy about by some means known only to himself—a prerogative well within the capacity of the Creator of the universe, whose works include not only galaxies but human cells. Nevertheless, the conception of Elizabeth's son, John the Baptizer, is attributed to God, to whom "nothing will be impossible" (Luke 1:37). Such was the habitual way of interpreting human events for devout people such as Elizabeth and Zechariah.

Again an understanding of the Holy Spirit is retrojected into the account; and rightly so, for it was within the purview of the inspired writer to interpret the events he was presenting in accord with spiritual realities, whether those realities were known to the characters involved or not. Elizabeth had no knowledge of the Holy Trinity, but that doesn't keep the Holy Spirit from motivating her response to Mary. Jesus and the Holy Spirit were also involved in creation, though the biblical accounts do not mention them with any specificity.[11]

Like Gabriel's greeting in the Annunciation, Elizabeth's greeting to the Blessed Virgin is part of the *Hail Mary*: "Blessed art thou among women, and blessed is the fruit of thy womb." To make up the completed prayer, the Church conflated the two greetings—Gabriel's and Elizabeth's—and added a petition based on the Communion of Saints, whose constant prayer for mortals bespeaks a loving solicitude for them and a burning desire for their salvation. The Blessed Mother, as Mother of the Lord and of all men, is especially asked to "pray for us sinners now and at the hour of our death." The Infancy Narrative is thus the source of the most important prayer, next to the *Our Father*, in Christendom.[12] The *Hail Mary* has formed a vital part of the spiritual life of untold millions of Catholics and Eastern Orthodox Christians. In recent years, even some Protestants have started praying the Rosary. Its roots are

---

[11] The Church Fathers taught extensively about the role of Jesus the Word in the Old Testament. St. Irenaeus, for instance, writes that Christ "is present with all those who were from the beginning approved by God, Who granted them His Word to be present with them. If any one, therefore, reads the Scriptures with attention, he will find in them an account of Christ, and a foreshadowing of the new calling" (*Against Heresies*, Book 4, chapters 25-26 [chapter heading omitted]).

[12] The first part of the *Hail Mary*, the combination of St. Gabriel's and St. Elizabeth's greetings to Our Lady ("Hail Mary, full of grace, the Lord is with thee. Blessed art thou among women and blessed is the fruit of thy womb, Jesus"), came into use for devotional purposes in the eleventh century. The second part ("Holy Mary, Mother of God, pray for us sinners now and at the hour of our death") did not come into universal use until the sixteenth century, when Pope St. Pius V included it in the new Roman breviary (1568).

Scripture, and it is deeply planted in the devotional sensibility of the people of God.

Mary joins Elizabeth in the "hill country" so that the two can rejoice together over the babies in their wombs. Again, the focus is on the unborn Christ. John leaps "with great joy" in the womb when Mary, carrying the Lord, enters the room. Elizabeth proclaims Mary "blessed among women" because of Christ and acknowledges that the visitor is the "mother of my Lord." She further paves the way for a proper devotion to the Blessed Virgin by praising Mary's faith in the Lord's promise. Thus in this famous scene the two women and the unborn Saint John are lenses through which we see the Lord; or, more literally, they are respondents to his presence. Unseen though he is, Jesus is the center of the story.

It is, incidentally, no breach of verisimilitude for Elizabeth to know already of Mary's pregnancy and of its mysterious origins. Time has elapsed since the Annunciation. Rumors have flown, for among kinsmen and rural people news travels rapidly; even today, in places where the extended family is still culturally important, there are no secrets among relatives. The news has spread: Mary is pregnant. Joseph has, one may presume, already accepted the miraculous origin of Christ's conception, of which he has been informed by "an angel of the Lord" (Matthew 1:20). The account of Elizabeth's words allows us to infer that she, like Joseph, has also become convinced of the divinity of Mary's child, never mind how. Since she knows of Mary's piety and purity, she can reach no other conclusion; to impute sin to Mary would be unthinkable. Elizabeth has recently seen God working in her own life in a most unexpected, perhaps miraculous, way, and, knowing Mary's character, she is aware that Mary's pregnancy must belong to an even higher order than her own—the order of immediate divine intervention.

Further context. The *Magnificat* is Mary's song of thanks to God. It is steeped in the traditions of ancient Hebrew poetry, in both form and thought. In form, the less important of the two categories, the song reflects to a high degree the parallelism and antithesis of the Psalms and other Old Testament poems. "My soul magnifies," for instance, is parallel to "my spirit rejoices." "The proud," "the mighty," and "the rich" are balanced against "the lowly" and "the hungry." The repetitive syntax—"He has shown," "he has scattered," "he has pulled down," "he has filled," "he has come to the aid"—builds the song toward its climactic reference to Abraham and the ancient covenant. Such repetition, far from producing monotony or mere redundancy, is a major artistic feature of Hebrew poetry and, through its influence, of English prose style, particularly in the seventeenth century, when "church English" flourished.

With regard to its content, the *Magnificat* belongs to an Old Testament class of poems (or songs) about the reversals that God causes in favor of his faithful servants. The Hebrews' chief axiom about the moral life is that God, the Creator and Lawgiver, has revealed his will to man. The next axiom, which is very often on the very surface of Sacred Scripture and never far below it, is that God rewards his servants and punishes those who rebel against him.[13] Out of this traditional understanding grows the justice that Mary expresses in the *Magnificat*: that the tables are turned, that the lowly have been rescued and the haughty demoted. There is plenty of precedent for this theme. Many psalms, for instance, deal with the idea of *rescue*. One good example, Psalm 124, includes a reflection that the Lord has rescued Israel from an unstated enemy,

---

[13] Cf. Deuteronomy 11:26-27: "Behold, I set before you this day a blessing and a curse: the blessing, if you obey the commandments of the Lord your God, which I command you this day, and the curse, if you do not obey the commandments of the Lord your God." See also Psalm 7:12: "A just judge is God, a God who punishes day by day." (New American Bible. The RSV has: "God is a righteous judge, and a God who has indignation every day.") This is the Deuteronomic law of negative retribution in a nutshell.

symbolized by a raging flood and fowlers who set traps: "We have escaped as a bird from the snare of the fowlers; the snare is broken, and we have escaped!"[14] The moral uprightness of the speaker who has been saved by God is always at least implied. In some psalms it is explicit: "When my enemies turned back, they stumbled and perished before thee. For thou hast maintained my just cause; thou hast sat on the throne giving righteous judgment" (Psalm 9:3-4).[15] Perhaps the most important Old Testament song in this genre is, significantly, that of a woman who seems very much like St. Elizabeth. Hannah, Samuel's mother, has been thought sterile. In the first chapter of 1 Samuel she prays earnestly for a child and promises to dedicate him to God. When her petition is granted, she sings in prayer a song that is now part of the Divine Office (1 Samuel 2). The language of this song shows that the imagery of the *Magnificat* was traditional long before Mary's time:

> My heart exults in the Lord;
> my strength is exalted in the Lord.
> My mouth derides my enemies,
> because I rejoice in thy salvation.

* * *

---

[14] Other rescue psalms abound—for instance, the great Psalm 18 and the liturgical hymn called Psalm 118.

[15] In many other psalms the speaker maintains his own righteousness. See, for instance, the beginning of Psalm 26: "Vindicate me, O Lord, for I have walked in my integrity … and I walk in faithfulness to thee." Psalm 17 is a wonderful statement of confidence in the eternal reward of God's servants, who are to awaken after the trials of life to see the face of God: "In justice shall behold your face; on waking, I shall be content in your presence" (verse 15, NAB). Such expressions of faith in transnatural justice are comparatively rare in the Old Testament, for most Old Testament observations on retribution are about earthly blessings. Though the idea of retribution is usually considered in negative terms, it is good to remember that the Scriptures contain hundreds of statements about the *positive* retribution (or reward) of those who serve the Lord.

The bows of the mighty are broken,
but the feeble gird on strength.
Those who were full have hired
themselves out for bread,
but those who were hungry have ceased to hunger.
The barren has borne seven
but she who has many children is forlorn.
The Lord kills and brings to life;
he brings down to Sheol and raises up.
The Lord makes poor and makes rich;
he brings low, he also exalts.

Though a previous condition of apparent barrenness is no part of the young Mary's life, she chooses to sing in the same mode as Hannah about how God looks with favor on the humble people who serve him.

The similarities between the songs are compelling. In both we find the rich demoted and the poor raised up, the fat brought to hunger and the hungry fed, the haughty deposed and the lowly exalted. More specific to the woman's role, both Mary and Hannah are rejoicing that they have been blessed with children. Hannah has lived under the stigma that attached to childless women in ancient Hebrew society and is rejoicing in the removal of that mark of shame. Mary, on the other hand, does not bear the demerit associated with barrenness. Nevertheless, she has become pregnant without being married and, in the eyes of her society, could be subject to horrible punishment if her condition became known.

That eventuality is prevented by the generosity of St. Joseph. Even before God communicates with Joseph, the carpenter of Nazareth shows himself a "just man" who is unwilling "to disgrace" Mary (Matthew 1:19). When the angel of the Lord does appear, Joseph listens to the announcement that the child developing in the Virgin's womb "is from the Holy Spirit" (Matthew 1:20)—that is, that Mary is indeed still a virgin. Joseph is thus invited to cooperate with God in the Incarnation, and like the Blessed Virgin he behaves with humble submission. We owe St. Joseph our thanks, for, like Mary, he facilitated God's Incarnation.

The *Magnificat* is, then, a traditional, artfully composed song that resembles many others in Scripture. But this fact does not destroy the verisimilitude of the Infancy Narrative. It is entirely plausible that the Blessed Mother, given time to reflect on what has happened, would sing such a song. She herself is depicted, especially in the story of the Presentation, as a pious young woman who readily obeys the law of God. (What other sort of mother would God choose?) It is only natural that one who interprets the events of her life in terms of her religion would employ the language of Scripture about the miraculous gift she has received. Similarly, St. John, for instance, uses apocalyptic language to describe the otherwise ineffable features of heaven. And furthermore, the inspiration of the Holy Spirit was surely accessible to his Bride: why should God not give eloquence to the Mother of the Word?

Zechariah, John the Baptizer's father, is also an important part of the scriptural context of the Visitation. He is a priest who, at or immediately before the time St. John is begotten, is on duty burning incense before the Temple veil. His wife, Elizabeth, is one of the "daughters of Aaron" (Luke 1:5). The two are "both righteous before God, blamelessly following all the commandments and regulations of the Lord" (Luke 1:6). Therefore the context of John's birth, parallel to that of the birth of Jesus, is a family that acknowledges the rulership of God and follows the divine laws. The parallelism, emphasized by the juxtaposition of Zechariah's canticle, the *Benedictus*, and the *Magnificat*, serves in itself to "magnify the Lord." Zechariah is focused on his own son at John's circumcision, not on the unborn Jesus. But his paternal pride centers on the fact that John is to "be called a prophet of the Most High," who "will go before the Lord to prepare his ways" (Luke 1:76). John's role in announcing the Lord is Zechariah's theme.

In this way Zechariah answers the questions of his neighbors, who have fallen into fear at the mystery of his inability to speak, and at the uncustomary naming of the child John when he has no relatives so named. Like Mary, these neighbors of Zechariah take to heart the portentous events surrounding the birth and look forward to finding out "What, then, will this child be?" (Luke 1:66). Zechariah's canticle tells them: the boy will preach the coming of that "dayspring" from heaven that will "give light to those who sit in darkness and in the shadow of death" (Luke 1:78-79). The Church in her Spirit-guided wisdom recognizes the beauty and spiritual value of the *Benedictus* and retains it in Morning Prayer of the Divine Office.

Extensions and applications. Mary's visit to Elizabeth is often cited as an example of selfless concern for another person. We see that the first thing Our Lady thinks of when she learns of Elizabeth's pregnancy is to visit and help her cousin. The two women then rejoice over the young lives in their wombs. They thus epitomize the immemorial custom of women who help each other in the task that most epitomizes and honors womanhood itself: bearing children. Men have no such important function, and their lives are often poorly spent if they don't orient themselves toward either the role of paterfamilias or the priesthood or religious life.

But the Visitation has further echoes in Scripture. The term *visit* itself connotes more than mere physical presence. When it is used in a positive sense, the Greek word translated "visit" in the New Testament also means "to inspect," "to care about (someone)," "to be solicitous about (someone)." The Septuagint (a widely used ancient Greek version of the Old Testament) employs the same usage. The psalmist asks in Psalm 8 (Douay translation), for instance, "What is man that thou art mindful of him, or the son of man that thou visitest him?" (The Revised Standard Version has "dost care" in place of "visitest.") In the parallel structure, "visitest" is equivalent to "art mindful." A *visit*, therefore, is in the first sense an expression of love and concern. God is said to visit man; when we act so as to express a similar concern for our fellows, we embody God's love. That is what the Blessed Virgin did when she visited Elizabeth.[16]

In the New Testament, visiting others is raised to a moral imperative. It is part of the social obligation of the Christian life. St. James, for instance, makes it an essential element of "pure religion": "Religion that is pure and undefiled in the eyes of God the Father is this: to visit orphans and widows in their distress, and to keep oneself unstained from the world" (James 1:27). In this passage St. James, whose letter is mainly devoted to insisting on the necessity of good works as well as faith, retains the negative moral norms in all their validity (keep yourself "unstained"), but adds to them the necessity of positive action. His admonition to visit those who need help carries with it the idea of meeting their needs, not merely of showing up. As God "visits" us in our distress, we become his instruments by visiting the afflicted, whether our purpose is to bring comfort through conversation, to supply food or other needs, or to bring the Eucharist.

Jesus makes the gravity of the obligation clear. According to our Lord's teaching, those who do not recognize him in the needy and respond to them accordingly will be sent to eternal punishment. At the Judgment Day,

---

[16] In the negative sense, a visit can be a curse. In the Old Testament when God "visits" someone, he brings either punishment or reward. The Lord says, for instance, that because the children of Israel have made a golden calf and worshiped it, he "will visit their sin upon them" (Exodus 32:34). That is, he is going to bring about the bad consequences of idolatry for those who have committed it.

he will say to those at his left hand, "Away from me, you cursed, into the eternal fire prepared for the devil and his angels; for I was hungry and you gave me no food, I was thirsty and you gave me no drink, I was a stranger and you did not take me in, naked and you did not clothe me, sick and in prison and you did not visit me.... Insofar as you did not do it for one of the least of these, you did not do it for me" (Matthew 25:41-43, 45).

In short, the entire scope of what is usually called the "works of mercy"[17] is comprehended in the biblical concept of visiting. These works are not optional for us. We ignore them at great peril to our souls.

A second application of the Visitation story to the modern world is its relevance to our attitude toward children. Many citizens of affluent nations have come to consider children a threat to their well-being or, at best, a troublesome blessing. This attitude is a natural extension of the radical individualism that materialists bring to bear on all moral decision-making.[18] Right and wrong are defined as subjective matters, determined by mutual consent, though some add the condition "as long as it doesn't hurt anyone."[19]

---

[17] The traditional list of *corporal* works of mercy: feeding the hungry, giving drink to the thirsty, clothing the naked, showing hospitality to strangers, visiting the sick, ministering to prisoners, and burying the dead. The *spiritual* works of mercy: converting the sinner, instructing the ignorant, counseling the doubtful, comforting the sorrowful, bearing wrongs patiently, forgiving injuries, and praying for the living and the dead.

[18] Cf. Germain Grisez, *The Way of the Lord Jesus*, Volume 2: *Living a Christian Life* (Quincy, IL: Franciscan Press, 1993), pp. 349-50, 353-56.

[19] In the absence of belief in the moral law and the God who gave it, mere consent has become more and more important as a pseudo-determiner of right and wrong. Whatever "consenting adults" want to do is considered okay. Consent, and consequently the morality of an action, therefore form just one more opinion in a world where every belief is just an opinion and every opinion is just as good as every other. Of course, consent does have objective moral significance: "full consent" is necessary for mortal sin to occur (see Germain Grisez, *The Way of the Lord Jesus*, Volume 1: *Christian Moral Principles* [Chicago: Franciscan Herald Press, 1983], pp. 365-367). But that is a different matter: in Christian teaching, consent to an intrinsically evil act makes one guilty of mortal sin, whereas in modern pagan teaching consent makes an evil act *right*. So far has our society strayed from the truth.

The fiction of consequenceless sin is a major premise of those who brought about the "sexual revolution." Paradoxically, however, they have devoted immense energy to *preventing* the natural consequences of their immorality—thus admitting that in the order of nature sexual sin does have repercussions. Even if pregnancy or disease are averted, these sins are not without their effect.[20] They shape the eternal destiny of the souls of their perpetrators and deprive the world of lives designed to do unique good works planned and desired by God.

Armed with legal and societal entitlements, radical materialists have been waging an unrelenting "war on population," to borrow a phrase from Jacqueline Kasun.[21] This war depends upon the same subjectivist and materialist attitude toward children as the sexual revolution. But—probably worse—much of the war effort is directed toward exporting that revolution to Third World countries. Nothing could be more foolish than the delusion that affluent nations such as the United States have the solution to most social problems. A few years ago, William Bennett attempted to formulate a set of measurements by which cultural decay could be estimated. According to the resulting *Index of Leading Cultural Indicators*, the United States is a world leader in the categories of divorce, illegitimacy, child abuse, abortion, single-female-headed families, crime, drug use, and television viewing, among other categories.[22] In the midst of great material prosperity, not to mention

---

[20] Grisez, *Living a Christian Life*, p. 664, states that "even solitary sexual sins are social sins insofar as they violate the body's capacity for self-giving and the sacramental significance of human sexuality." Every impure act, even if solitary, deprives the world of the goodness God meant it to have.

[21] The hysteria, lies, and political power of opponents of population growth are thoroughly and brilliantly presented in Jacqueline Kasun's *The War Against Population* (San Francisco: Ignatius Press, 1988).

[22] William J. Bennett, *The Index of Leading Cultural Indicators* (Washington, DC: Heritage Foundation, *et al.*, 1993).

great claims to faith in God and Christ, the United States and other materially developed nations through such agencies as the United Nations, as well as by more direct means, seem determined to export as much wrongdoing—contraception, abortion, sterilization, divorce—as possible.

This effort is based on one of the most widely accepted myths of modern times, the myth of overpopulation.[23] It is buoyed up by constant attacks upon the institution of the family. The family is, after all, the natural enemy of radical individualism. It embodies a first principle of Christian anthropology, that individuals are not and cannot be totally autonomous, but are dependent upon each other. As we exist in an I-Thou relationship with God, we live in an I-thou relationship with each other, especially in the family.

Although only too eager to export our own cultural evils, American social engineers resent any effort to take Christ to places that have not heard the Gospel. To them, missionary work is "cultural imperialism," an unjustified attempt to foist one's own cultural traits off on innocent foreigners. And yet, through such institutions as the International Planned Parenthood Federation, and with money from multinational organizations as bait and blackmail, they push condoms, IUDs, and, especially, abortion and sterilization upon Third World people. Recent "women's" meetings

---

[23] Although Thomas Malthus, grandfather of the "population bomb" theory, was long ago proved wrong, his modern followers continue to scare gullible people and command the resources and energy of huge international organizations such as the United Nations. The International Planned Parenthood Federation relies heavily on the myth of overpopulation to promote abortion and contraception. The United States is the world's largest promoter of these evils. The idea that population growth cannot be "sustained" (an antilife buzzword) and the accompanying delusion that people starve merely because they exist are so deeply ingrained in the modern sensibility that almost no one recognizes them as uncritically accepted dogmas. With them we accept the false notion that we are compelled to contraception and abortion. But God has promised that he will help us so that we need not sin no matter what problems we encounter. Much of the "need" to sin is just a ticket to self-indulgence.

such as those at Cairo and Beijing were fundamentally designed to move the world closer to acceptance of a total anti-family ethic.[24]

Nothing could be further, however, from the lessons of the Visitation. The Virgin's visit itself negates radical individualism and bespeaks self-sacrifice. Her purpose is to share Elizabeth's joy at the coming birth, a joy that is incomprehensible to the radical-individualist ethos, which sees only a burden in children. The whole scene, in addition to its focus on Jesus as the Son of God, teaches that children are a gift from God and should be accepted as such with joy and gratitude. The underlying idea of self-giving foreshadows the Lord's total gift of himself on Calvary.

Mary's joy in the Visitation. Though already unbounded, Elizabeth's joy at the prospect of having a child was increased by the arrival of her cousin, the Mother of her Lord. The mystery of the Incarnation continued to unfold for Mary, as she saw the effect her arrival had upon Elizabeth and John. Then both women, with great rejoicing, remained together in mutual charity and holy expectation until just about the time for Elizabeth's delivery.

Suggested intentions. Mary and Elizabeth derived great joy from the young lives within them. In our age of spiritual pride, we have actually presumed to define the lives of the unborn out of existence. As a society we lie to ourselves and say that the unborn are not really human in the fullest sense, or that for some odd reason the "rights" of a mother cancel her child's basic right to life.

---

[24] At the recent conferences in Cairo and Beijing the antilife armories of the United States and the United Nations took the field against the Church and the world's traditional societies. For an introduction to these conferences, see George Weigel, "What Really Happened at Cairo," *First Things*, February 1995, pp. 24-31, and Mary Ann Glendon, "What Happened at Beijing," *First Things*, January 1996, pp. 30-36.

We can offer this decade of the Rosary for the conversion of our world—for an end to contraceptivism in the broad sense, which includes abortion and the war on children and population. Affirmatively, we can pray for the beginning of a new culture of life and love.

3

THE NATIVITY

Littera: Scripture and gloss. Neither St. Mark nor St. John gives an account of the birth of Christ. St. Matthew's account of the birth itself, as opposed to the incidents that preceded it (see below) is quite abbreviated. The fullest record is that of St. Luke, where most of the Infancy Narrative is found:

> Now it happened that in those days a decree went out from Caesar Augustus that all the world should be registered. This first registration took place when Quirinius was governor of Syria. So everyone went to be registered, each to his own city. Since Joseph was of the house and family of David he went up from Nazareth in Galilee to Bethlehem of Judea, the city of David, to be registered with Mary, who was betrothed to him and who was pregnant. Now it happened that while they were there, the days for her to give birth were fulfilled. She gave birth to her firstborn son, wrapped him in swaddling cloths, and laid him in a manger, because there was no room for them in the inn (Luke 2:1-7).

St. Luke evidently has two main purposes in giving this account of the Nativity: he wanted (1) to tell why Jesus was born in Bethlehem, and (2) to present the birth itself and some features that surround it. The first purpose is fulfilled by an account of the historical circumstances of Joseph's journey to Bethlehem. Joseph belongs to the "house and family" or lineage of King David and so must go to Bethlehem, the "city of David," to be enrolled in the census ordered by the emperor of Rome, Augustus. The second purpose is accomplished with great brevity but with significant detail. The inn was full, so Joseph and Mary stayed in a stable, where the child was born. When he was wrapped (swaddled) in cloth, he was laid in a manger, the only crib-like furnishing available. The hay in the manger would have provided some softness; perhaps most of the beds ever made in the history of the world have been filled with straw (though people have probably more often slept without actual beds).

The account of the Annunciation emphasized that David was the prototype of Jesus. The lineage of Joseph brings the Holy Family to Bethlehem and so makes Jesus' birth in the city of David a reality. Thus Luke records the features of Christ's birth that make the Nativity a fulfillment of Scripture, though he doesn't specifically say so. As usual, St. Matthew is more explicit about prophecy:

> Now the birth of Jesus Christ came about like this. When his Mother Mary was betrothed to Joseph, but before they came together, she was found to be with child by the Holy Spirit. Joseph, her husband, was a good and upright man so he was planning to put her away, but quietly because he didn't want to disgrace her. But while he was thinking these things over, behold, the angel of the Lord appeared to him in a dream and said, "Joseph, son of David, don't be afraid to take your wife Mary into your house—the child who has been conceived in her is from the Holy Spirit. She will give birth to a son and you shall name him Jesus, because he will save his people from their sins." All this took place to fulfill what was declared by the Lord through the prophet when he said: "Behold, the virgin shall be with child and will give birth to a son, and they shall give him the name Emmanuel," which is translated, "God with us" (Matthew 1:13-23).

Matthew is writing for an audience familiar with the Scriptures and eager for their fulfillment—that is, primarily a Jewish audience. A good deal of his presentation of the life and sayings of Christ is therefore devoted to showing how Jesus is the Messiah foretold by Old Testament prophecy. Luke is just as interested in Jesus as the Messiah, but is less concerned to prove the point scripturally.

Further context. And so the child Jesus was born. God had become man in the same form we all bear into the world—that of a tiny, wet, totally dependent infant pulling behind him the cord by which he was fastened to his Mother's womb. No midwife is mentioned. His foster father must have picked him up and placed him in Mary's arms. His first sensations must have been the chill of the winter night air, the smells of hay and manure, the rough, just, kind hands of the carpenter Joseph, and the comforting sounds of his Mother's voice. Greater condescension than this would be hard to imagine: that God the Creator not only becomes part of his creation, but that he does so in such a homely fashion, not as an earthly ruler or man of wealth, but as the least member of a family without much influence or money, who couldn't even command a hotel room. People speak of the poverty of the Holy Family, though in worldly terms Joseph and Mary were not absolutely poor; Joseph was known for his craft and was not destitute. But no greater example of what is called *spiritual* poverty could be imagined.[25] God humbles himself and becomes subject to all the features of an unpresuming human infancy—birth into a family that gets no special treatment, birth in a stable with its accoutrements of cold and smells, taking his first sleep in a trough of animal feed.

So began God's life outside the womb of his Mother. He, like

---

[25] C.S. Lewis, in a simile meant to describe the great distance to which God descends to become a man, likens the Incarnation to a human being's becoming "a slug or a crab" (*Mere Christianity*, rev. ed., New York: Macmillan, 1985, p. 140). But of course he knew that the actual distance is much greater.

all babies soon after their conception, had already become passible—capable of receiving sense impressions and therefore capable of suffering. Now, his life began to take on an entirely new dimension. The whole venture of God into his own creation, which we call the Incarnation, was undertaken so that God could suffer, for in his omnipotence outside the created universe he was completely active, not acted upon. The man Jesus is the passible member of the Holy Trinity. Only he—not the Father and not the Holy Spirit—can have what human beings call *experience*. In him, God who created everything becomes a part of the complex web of causes and effects that we call nature. In becoming man, Jesus became the object of causes rather than their principle or beginning. In him God becomes capable of *undergoing*. The cold night air made the Divine Baby shiver.

The Incarnation unfolds before us as a progressive public revelation that begins with the Annunciation and ends with the events of the book of Acts and the theological, pastoral, and eschatological reflections of the inspired New Testament writers. The Incarnation is foretold in the Old Testament under a symbolic veil. It is revealed to Mary, then to Joseph, then to Elizabeth, then to the shepherds and wise men, and subsequently to Holy Simeon and Holy Anna in the Temple. Its mystery unfolds bafflingly to Mary and Joseph when Jesus is found uttering wisdom in the Temple at the age of twelve. And so on, through the preaching of St. John the Baptizer, to the public ministry of the Lord with his divine teaching and miraculous signs, to his death and the greatest signs of all: his Resurrection and his continued presence in the Church, in the holy Eucharist and the Magisterium,[26] as well as in the rightly

---

[26] We rightly think of the Holy Spirit as guiding the Magisterium of the Church. But, as St. Augustine points out, when one member of the Holy Trinity is named, "the Persons [are] also each severally named; and yet are not to be understood as though the other Persons were excluded, on account of the unity of the same Trinity and the One sub-

formed Christian conscience. The Nativity is a profound step in this revelation: Christ, nurtured under the Virgin's heart, leaves the protection of his Mother's womb to begin a more perilous life, to be followed as a teacher from God, honored as a king, then reviled as a blasphemer and executed as a criminal. The symbols of Christ's passion appear in icons of his infancy: the cross, for example, adorns the picture of Our Lady of Perpetual Help. In the adversities of his birth are adumbrated the redemptive acts of his life. Small wonder the Christian world worships at his manger.

Extensions and applications. I have spoken of the spiritual motherhood of Mary—the fact that she in becoming the Mother of Christ became the Mother of all human beings. Because "in a wholly singular way she cooperated by her obedience, faith, hope and burning charity in the work of the Savior in restoring supernatural life to souls... she is a Mother to us in the order of grace."[27] In celebrating the Nativity the Church "both adores the Savior and venerates His glorious Mother."[28] As we recognize her motherhood, we realize that she is capable of bringing Jesus to birth in all of us. As God requested, she nourished and shaped the Prototype in her body—the very form of virtue, of conformity to the will of the Father, who, though of the same substance as the Father, took "the form of a servant ... and became obedient unto death" (Philippians 2:7,8). She will help *us* through her maternal inter-

---

stance and Godhead of the Father and of the Son and of the Holy Spirit" (*On the Trinity*, Bk. 1, Ch. 9; *Basic Writings of St. Augustine*, ed. Whitney J. Oates [New York: Random House, 1948], Volume 2, p. 684). Though Jesus alone is perfect God and perfect Man, Augustine clearly teaches that seeing him is the equivalent of seeing the Father. The guidance of the Holy Spirit is likewise the guidance of Christ, whom the Fathers perceived in the entire spiritual history of Israel and who promised to be with the Church until the end of time (Matthew 28:20).

[27] *Lumen Gentium*, no. 62.

[28] Pope Paul VI, *Marialis Cultus*, no. 5.

cession to follow that pattern of obedience. Thus she will bring the image of Christ to birth in our lives, if we will only ask her to help us, like the Firstborn, to know and do the will of the Father. If we submit to her, the motherhood of Mary brings Jesus to birth in us and us to birth in him.

Supernatural phenomena such as the song of the angels aside, the earthly circumstances of Christ's birth were perfectly ordinary: taxes, censuses, travel on a donkey (a standard mode of conveyance for unimportant but not destitute people until deep into the twentieth century), a crowded town, uncomfortable and lowly lodging, a young woman giving birth. God calls Joseph to Bethlehem through a decree of Caesar. That fact gets Mary to the city of David, where prophecy states that the Messiah is to be born. As far as we can see, the Father works through such secondary causes most of the time; when he wants us to go somewhere, he usually prompts us to do so by worldly means, not by direct intervention. The entrance of the Divine Word into the world could have been accomplished by other means than the ones God chose, though it would seem that without a human birth the Lord would not have been fully human. God chooses, however, to use ordinary bodily processes and natural, even political, means to carry out his will. That fact gives great spiritual significance to ordinary life, for it tells us that ordinary life is the field in which we must seek to know and do God's will.

No saint has taught more clearly or appealingly on this matter than St. Thérèse of Lisieux, who knew that the minute conflicts and superficially trivial events of daily life are filled with moral significance. She writes in her *Autobiography*, for instance, "[I]f, when I am preparing for some work, I find that the brushes and the paints are in disorder, if a rule or a penknife has disappeared, patience is very close to abandoning me and I must take my courage in both hands in order to reclaim the missing object without

bitterness."[29] The intensity of her moral and spiritual vision en-
lightened her about the meaning of life. Moral struggle, she realized, generally takes place in daily trivia. Partly because of this
moral realism, which is an aspect of her great self-abnegation, St.
Thérèse was able in her abbreviated life to achieve the greatest
sanctity.

Mary's joy in the Nativity. The birth of Jesus in the stable
at Bethlehem, together with the excitement it caused among the
angels, shepherds, wise men, and fools, was in a sense the culmination of the Annunciation. Mary and Joseph shared the joy of
seeing at last the baby whose conception had been so mysterious
and so portentous. Herod, in a savage fit of paranoia, sealed the
doom of the Holy Innocents. And with joy the Blessed Virgin
started caring for the new human being who had been entrusted
to her. Such an embarkation should always be filled with wonder,
humility, and joy; how much more so when the new child was the
Lord.

Suggested intentions. Because interpersonal connections are
so much a part of the spirituality of ordinary life, and because all
of us have exerted both good and bad influence in our own interpersonal relationships, we should pray for all who have touched
our lives and whose lives we have touched, especially those we have
hurt unnecessarily or influenced for evil. Thus we can bring Christ
to birth in ourselves and our society.

---

[29] *Story of a Soul: the Autobiography of St. Thérèse of Lisieux*, trans. John Clarke, O.C.D.
(Washington: Institute of Carmelite Studies, 1975), p. 226.

4

THE PRESENTATION

Littera: Scripture and gloss. The biblical account of the Presentation comes from the Infancy Narrative in St. Luke:

> When the days of their purification according to the law of Moses had passed, they took the child up to Jerusalem to present him to the Lord—as it is written in the law of the Lord, "Every firstborn male shall be called holy to the Lord"—and to offer a sacrifice according to what is said in the law of the Lord, "a pair of turtledoves, or two young pigeons."
>
> And, behold, there was a man in Jerusalem named Simeon. He was an upright and devout man who awaited the liberation of Israel, and the Holy Spirit was upon him; moreover it had been revealed to him by the Holy Spirit that he would not see death before he had seen the Messiah of the Lord. He was led by the Spirit to come to the Temple and when the parents brought the child Jesus in to do for him according to the custom of the law, he took him in his arms and blessed God, saying,
>
> "Now You send Your servant away in peace, O Lord,
>   according to Your word;
>   because my eyes have seen Your salvation
>   prepared in the presence of all the peoples,
>   a light of revelation to the Gentiles,
>   and glory to Your people Israel."
>
> His father and his Mother were amazed at what was said about Jesus. And Simeon blessed them and said to his mother, Mary, "Behold, this child is destined to bring about the fall

and rise of many in Israel,
and to be a sign that will be opposed;
And a sword will pierce your own soul,
so that thoughts of many hearts
may be revealed."

The prophetess Anna was there, too, the daughter of
Phanuel from the tribe of Asher; she was greatly advanced
in years, having lived seven years with her husband from
her virginity, and alone as a widow till she was eighty-four,
worshiping night and day in the Temple with fasting and
prayer. And she came up at that very hour and began to
give thanks to God and spoke about him to all who were
awaiting the liberation of Israel.

When they had carried out everything according to
the law of the Lord, they returned into Galilee to their own
city, Nazareth. And the child grew and became strong and
was filled with wisdom; and the grace of God was on him
(Luke 2:22-40).

The *law* is mentioned five times in this short passage. Though
the focus is on the child Jesus and the reception he gets in the
Temple, the cause of his being brought there is clearly emphasized:
Joseph and Mary are obeying the law of Moses. The law that compelled them, stated in Leviticus 12, declares a woman who has
borne a child to be "unclean"; this should be clearly understood as
a *ritual* uncleanness, however, not a moral one. What it amounts
to is a ritual requirement that a certain time pass and that certain
sacrifices be made after the birth. It further requires that a male
child be circumcised on the eighth day after his birth, after which
the mother must wait a certain time before entering the Temple.
Fulfilling the requirement of circumcision amounts to a clear statement that the new baby is included in the ancient covenant that
God made with Abraham. Why God chose circumcision as the sign
of the covenant is a mystery whose rationale is known only to him.
Though circumcision is sometimes considered to be for the pur-

pose of hygiene, no one really knows why, aside from God's revealed command, this strange surgical ritual became a mark of the covenant. But it did so, and the Jews have adhered to the practice through the ages. Moreover, ancient Israel internalized the physical sign and gave it symbolic meaning. The realization that circumcision can be a mere external sign without internal significance reaches as far back as Deuteronomy, where love of God is equated to circumcision of heart: "the Lord your God will circumcise your heart and the heart of your offspring, so that you will love the Lord your God with all your heart and with all your soul, that you may live" (Deuteronomy 30:6). Elaborating on the exhortations in Deuteronomy to "circumcise ... the foreskin of your heart" (Deuteronomy 10:16), St. Paul uses circumcision as a metaphor for internal conversion and states that by itself the external sign is meaningless: "we are the true circumcision, who worship God in spirit, and glory in Christ Jesus, and put no confidence in the flesh" (Philippians 3:3). But the main reason for the circumcision of Christ in the Presentation story is simply that the law commands it.

In the entire Presentation is latent the attitude that inspired the author of Psalm 119, which is a protracted paean on God's law. "At midnight I rise to praise thee," he writes, "because of thy righteous ordinances" (verse 62). In our rebellion against God, all too often we resent his governance and accept it with clenched teeth. But here sings a servant of the Lord who praises him *because of* his ordinances, not in spite of them.

The law further decrees—and is quoted by St. Luke here— that every male child, especially the firstborn, is holy to the Lord and must be consecrated to him (Exodus 13:2). The *presentation* of the child to God fulfills this command. With the presentation goes the sacrifice of "a lamb a year old for a burnt offering, and a young pigeon or a turtledove for a sin offering" (Leviticus 12:6). The law further states that if the mother "cannot afford a lamb, then she shall take two turtledoves or two young pigeons, one for a burnt offering and the other for a sin offering; and the priest shall make atonement for her, and she shall be clean" (Leviticus 12:8). It is noteworthy that if the Blessed Virgin offers a sin offering, it is not because she has sinned; like the later offering of Christ on the cross—the definitive sin offering—it is not made for herself. It is also a sign of the social and economic status of the Holy Family that Joseph and Mary have to offer the less expensive sacrifice.

The other characters in the Presentation story, Simeon and Anna, marvelously enhance the focus on Christ. Simeon had been waiting for the "liberation of Israel," i.e., the coming of the Messiah. Anna speaks with enthusiasm about the baby Jesus to others who, like herself, "were [also] looking for the liberation of Israel." Simeon comes to the Temple at the prompting of the Holy Spirit, perhaps aware that now his years of waiting will be repaid. When he sees the Lord, he rejoices and utters a prayer of great peace and confidence, the *Nunc Dimittis*. Simeon knows nothing of the details of the Lord's coming ministry, yet he responds with faith. Even Mary herself is often baffled and must ponder the actions of her divine Son. Nor do we know where our faith in Christ will take us—what the future details of our personal vocations will be. Simeon's prayer suggests that he has received the consolation that he has sought for the Jewish people. One may well wish that Anna's words were recorded: what did she say to the others who, like herself, had not compromised their faith or quenched it in worldly affairs, but sought and prayed for the "liberation" that was to come?

Finally, Simeon utters two dark prophecies about the child: that he will be "a sign that will be opposed" and that opposition to him will become a sword that pierces his Mother's soul. Like the other Joyful Mysteries, especially the Finding in the Temple, the Presentation is not a story of unmixed joy, for the words of Simeon adumbrate both Christ's pain and the division that his mission of salvation will bring. Jesus comes as the Prince of Peace (Isaiah 9:6), but his coming also brings strife between those who accept him and those who do not. That is true not only of Israel, as in Simeon's words, but also of families throughout the Christian world. "Do not think that I came to bring peace on earth," says the Lord. "I came not to bring peace, but a sword. For I came to turn a man against his father, and a daughter against her mother, and a daughter-in-law against her mother-in-law; and a man's enemies will be the members of his own household" (Matthew 10:35-36). Christ is a "'stone that they will trip over, a rock that they will stumble on'; they stumble because they disobey the word—as they were born to do" (1 Peter 2:8). Though followers of Christ can have great internal peace even in the heat of war or disease, faith in him causes resentment and hostility among his opponents. *Odium fidei,* "hatred of the faith," is alive and well in the world today. For the enemies of Christ, the Christian is also a "sign that will be opposed." The great difficulty for Christians is twofold: (1) they must often accept the hostility of their associates or even of their own families, and (2) they face the constant temptation to return evil for evil, an exchange that would reduce them to the level of Christ's enemies. We must never give in to the temptation to hate the enemies of the Lord and return their hostility. Rather, we must pray always for their conversion, set them the best example possible, let them know that we care about them, and keep in mind the prayer of Christ on the cross: "Father, forgive them; for they know not what they do" (Luke 23:34). That "best example" should include no self-righteousness about our own religious practices, and none of the self-pitying drama of flaunted martyrdom.

Further context. The "consolation" and "redemption" that Simeon and Anna are so eager to see is the equivalent of the expectation of the Messiah discussed above under the Annunciation. The fact that they recognize the fulfillment of their expectation in Jesus means that they see the ancient covenant fulfilled in him.

Extensions and applications. The *Nunc Dimittis*, Holy Simeon's prayer, is used in the night prayer (Compline) of the Divine Office, the daily prayer of the Church. It is an expression to God of acceptance of death and of confidence in the fullness of his grace. Simeon's hope for the coming "liberation of Israel" had been heightened by God himself, for "it had been revealed to him by the Holy Spirit that he would not see death before he had seen the Messiah of the Lord." His prayer is a reflection on the sufficiency of his life, brought to a full realization at the Presentation: he has indeed seen the child who is a "light of revelation to the Gentiles and glory to [God's] people Israel." Consequently, Simeon is ready to die, or be "sent away," in great peace. This prayer grows profounder with usage, as one comes to see its application to the Christian life. It would be hard to imagine a better way of ending a day: in the Divine Office, God's servant examines his conscience, expresses sorrow for his sin, entrusts himself to God in the words of Christ: "*In manus tuas, Domine, commendo spiritum meum*": "Father, into your hands I entrust my spirit!" (Luke 23:46, quoting Psalm 31:5). He then recites Holy Simeon's canticle. In the context of Compline, the *Nunc Dimittis* becomes a night song of gratitude for the salvation brought by Christ, as well as an expression of acceptance and contentment with God's great bounty and with whatever happens next—even if it is death. We know the Lord, says this prayer, and that is enough for us. Bedtime has always been a symbol for death-time, and rightly so. We relinquish conscious control of our bodies and minds and entrust ourselves to the Father in order to rise refreshed—now day by day, night by night, morning by freely given morning; but before long we will lie down in a definitive sleep that leads to an everlasting dawn. We should always live in such a way that Holy Simeon's attitude toward death can be ours. In Jesus we need not fear that sleep.

The sword about which Simeon speaks is a symbol of the pain that the Blessed Virgin is to endure because of Christ. Just as in the Incarnation she becomes the Mother of every Christian, Jesus becomes the type of every child who embodies his parents' hopes and consequently their fears, desires, and pain. To see those hopes dashed on Calvary is the ultimate suffering. The sword pierces our Mother's heart as we stand with her at the foot of the cross. In her empathy with Jesus, as in her *fiat mihi* spoken to the angel of the Annunciation—indeed, as a consequence of her cooperation with the Holy Spirit—the Blessed Virgin becomes the proto-Christian. As such she is an exponent of the Epiphany, not only at the Nativity and in the Presentation but later at the wedding in Cana of Galilee. (She has no obvious role in the baptism of Jesus, traditionally part of the Epiphany.) Speaking about Jesus, her astonishing and mysterious Son, she tells the wedding servants to "do whatever he tells you" (John 1:5). These words, the last recorded utterance of the Blessed Virgin, stand as a permanent injunction to all Christians, for whom she is a model.

But she is not a model of a painless life—a fact that is amply emphasized even in the Presentation. In fact, Simeon's dark prophecy makes the Presentation, one of the Joyful Mysteries, also one of the Seven Sorrows of the Blessed Virgin. Pope Leo XIII emphasizes the intrinsic link between the Presentation and the Crucifixion: "that He might before men offer Himself as a victim to His Heavenly Father, He desires to be taken to the Temple; and by the hands of Mary He is there presented to the Lord."[30] Pope Paul VI points out that Mary's role is that of the "Virgin presenting offerings." The sorrow of separation between Mother and Son is combined with Mary's knowledge that she is transcending the requirements of the law. (She offers both the required animal sacrifice and her Son.) Simeon's words "came true on Calvary." The Presentation is therefore oriented "to the salvific event of the

---

[30] Pope Leo XIII, *Iucunda Semper Expectatione* (On the Rosary), September 8, 1894, no. 2.

cross." Moreover, the Church sees "in the heart of the Virgin … a desire to make an offering, a desire that exceeds the ordinary meaning of the rite." She offers "for the reconciliation of us all the holy Victim which is pleasing to God,"[31] thus making the Presentation "a mystery in which the Blessed Virgin was intimately associated as the Mother of the Suffering Servant of Yahweh, as the one who performs a mission belonging to ancient Israel, and as the model for the new People of God."[32]

As we emulate her devotion and vicariously experience the Joyful Mysteries, we look through the eyes of the loving Mother who eventually sees her perfect Son rejected and killed. It is because of her empathy that the Sorrowful Mysteries, foreshadowed in the Presentation, are *hers*: Jesus suffers the physical pain, but his Mother suffers equally great pain of heart. It was Mary's freely accepted lot to bear a Son whose divine mission she at first only dimly foresaw; surely not until after the Resurrection and Pentecost did she fully understand. Before that glorious triumph, she must come to know that her divine child was not to be a carpenter like his foster father but a prophet whose zeal for the Father's works led to rejection and death. His very goodness brings his Passion. In the last two Joyful Mysteries Mary hears ominous words to ponder, to puzzle over, as she becomes increasingly aware of the price that God is to pay for becoming human and of her own expense as his Mother. The Blessed Mother therefore lives for years in her own Gethsemane, in which she sees the inexorable progress of Jesus toward seeming failure and death. She shares his rejection, his thwarted hopes, his apparent failure, and his dread of torture: these are key elements of the Lord's Agony in Gethsemane, which is itself the prelude to Golgotha. This is one of the meanings of "let it

---

[31] Pope Paul VI, *Marialis Cultus*, no. 20. The last clause is a quotation from St. Bernard.
[32] *Ibid.*, no. 7.

be done to me according to your word" (Luke 1:38): great sorrow and blind, stupefying pain, before final joy. A prolonged sword-thrust indeed, vaguely foretold by the disturbing words of Holy Simeon.

Another extension of the Presentation is what might be called its symbolic family meaning. I once heard a lecture on biblical archetypes by a Jungian psychologist who was also a Christian. An archetype is a quintessential example of human experience, often a mythological figure who embodies deep human meaning and whose actions epitomize universal human experience. The search for archetypes has, however, led to some very unlikely interpretations both of Scripture and of Christian art—especially architecture. This is only natural, since Jung was hardly a theologian. Nevertheless, one aspect of the Presentation has all of the force of a symbolic action recapitulated throughout human history and embedded deeply in the human psyche. If any archetypes exist in Scripture, surely the picture of a young mother presenting her newborn son to his father is one. Just as the patient and serene St. Joseph laid the newborn Jesus in Mary's arms, Mary takes the Child to his real Father's house and presents him there to the Creator who engendered him in her body. She also presents him to the world as she presents him to his Father.

The large significance of law in the Presentation leads to a final extension. I have stated that in the biblical account, law is mentioned five times. The law given to Moses at Sinai, recorded in the book of Exodus, and elaborated and repeated in the rest of the Pentateuch, was the defining feature of the chosen people; they would not have been a people without it. The law spelled out a transcendent duty for the Jews and consequently for the Holy Family. From early childhood, long before he begins his public ministry, Jesus is steeped in the language and substance of the Mosaic law—which is, after all, the revelation of his Father. Jesus is the fulfillment of that law, as he teaches (Matthew 5:17). Because of this, his Incarnation involves immersion in Jewish culture and its modes of thought, its vocabulary. It is small wonder that he quotes the Pentateuch so often,[33] for these books embody the revelation of the Father to the chosen people, among whom Joseph and Mary shine as examples of obedience. It is no accident that the Son of God is born not only to an immaculately conceived Mother, but to a Mother who knows the law and obeys it implicitly; for the law is the preparation for the Son's work.[34] The Son, in his turn, negates none of the divine law, though he rejects merely human accretions to it and abuses of it. On the contrary, he not only retains the ancient moral precepts but deepens them by showing how they are grounded in nature, revealed by the Father, and necessary for salvation. The Son, who is truth, can reject none of the truth. He can only reveal it in greater depth.[35]

Mary at the Presentation. We often respond to laws and requirements with something like, "Aw, do I *have* to?" One of the most noteworthy features of the Presentation, however, is that it

---

[33] See, for instance, Matthew 2:34-40, where Jesus quotes Leviticus and Deuteronomy on the subject of love for God and one's neighbor.

[34] See Galatians 3:23-26: "Now before faith came, we were confined under the law, kept under restraint until faith should be revealed. So that the law was our custodian until Christ came, that we might be justified by faith. But now that faith has come, we are no longer under a custodian; for in Christ Jesus you are all sons of God, through faith." Older versions read "schoolmaster" instead of "custodian"; I prefer the older term, since the latter now suggests "janitor." In either case, St. Paul presents the Mosaic law as a means of preparing God's people for the coming of the Anointed One, who continues God's revelation. Jesus transforms the legal strictures of the Pentateuch by revealing that they protect basic human goods. These laws cannot be abrogated. See Grisez, *Christian Moral Principles*, pp. 920-921 s.v. *goods*, and the passages referred to there.

[35] Pope John Paul II's great encyclical on truth, *Veritatis Splendor*, insists on the objective reality of moral truth, in the face of a hostile world that has formally embraced relativism. The Holy Father stands bravely up like his ultimate predecessor, St. Peter, against a world that has jettisoned its own moral rudder. I suspect that nobody actually believes in relativism in its radical form. Like the appeal to consent for moral authority, the claim that all "truth" is relative is generally a way of giving oneself permission to do as one pleases. When someone else transgresses, however, a higher principle is adduced.

combines obedience with joy. That is, rather than being an "onerous mystery" about a duty grudgingly undertaken merely because it is a duty, the Presentation is a joyful mystery about how obedience to the law of God was a joy to Our Lady. There is much to imitate there. Add that fact to her innocent maternal pride in her new Son, and the result is unbounded joy for her.

Suggested intentions. We should pray that as the Mother of God presented her Firstborn to his Father in the Temple, she will continue to present *us*, her younger children, to the Creator by her maternal care and intercession. As she carried out the Presentation in obedience to the law of God, we should pray that we may genuinely love that law. Finally, as love of the law of God is the beginning of wisdom, we should pray for a true renewal of wisdom both in the Church and in society at large. Thus will come about a genuine renewal of Holy Mother Church—an intention for which we can offer this mystery.

5

THE FINDING IN THE TEMPLE

Littera: Scripture and gloss. Luke 2:41-52 reads:

> His parents used to go to Jerusalem every year for the
> festival of the Passover. And when he was about to turn
> twelve, they went up according to custom; and after the
> feast had ended, while they were returning, the child Jesus
> remained in Jerusalem, and his parents did not know it.
> Since they thought he was in their group of travelers they
> went a day's journey, and then looked for him among their
> relatives and acquaintances; and when they did not find
> him, they returned to Jerusalem in search of him. Now it
> happened that after three days they found him in the
> Temple, seated in the midst of the teachers, both listening
> to them and asking them questions; and all who heard him
> were amazed at his intelligence and his answers. And when
> his parents saw him they were astonished, and his mother
> said to him, "Son, why did you do this to us? You see your
> father and I have been looking for you and worrying." And
> he said to them, "Why were you looking for me? Did you
> not know that I have to concern myself with my Father's
> affairs?" And they did not understand what he was telling
> them. Then he went down with them and came to
> Nazareth, and he was subject to them. His mother kept
> all these things in her heart, and Jesus progressed in
> wisdom and age and grace before God and men.

Though many more or less fanciful stories about the childhood of Jesus occur in non-scriptural sources, the Finding in the

Temple is the only biblical episode about the subject. We are told nothing else directly in canonical sources about the life of Christ between his infancy and the beginning of his public ministry. Nevertheless, what the story does tell us suggests a great deal about the human development of the Lord—a subject to which I will return.

The Scripture presents a contrast between Jesus, whose conscious action sets off a frantic search, and Mary and Joseph, who at first react with little understanding but are led to new knowledge and new amazement at the Divine Child's actions. St. Luke states that Jesus "remained in Jerusalem." The Divine Child has evidently been allowed considerable freedom between his birth and this stage. Joseph and Mary assume without anxiety that Jesus is in the caravan, a fact that suggests they don't try to control him much or worry about him. There is no hint that Jesus' staying behind was accidental. It seems to have been a perfectly deliberate decision on his part. And so he was never "lost," at least from his own point of view, but was engaged in a rational activity that his parents, as he suggests, should have foreseen. Their lack of understanding implies that they have not been preoccupied with the mysterious, divine origin of their Son; life in Nazareth with him has been deceptively uneventful.[36] It is as if the supernatural mode of Christ's conception were forgotten and then reintroduced in this passage. Jesus recalls Mary and Joseph to the reality of his origin by stating that he had "to concern [himself] with [his] Father's affairs." He suggests, without insult or disrespect, that they have ignorantly searched elsewhere. This is why the search took three

---

[36] Some of the imaginative stories of Christ's childhood—e.g., a medieval English one in which He makes birds of mud and brings them to life—are far from the mark of Scripture. If Joseph and Mary had been accustomed to such daily miracles at home, they would hardly have been surprised at anything Jesus did. I imagine that, except for his moral perfection and preternatural understanding, Jesus seemed an ordinary boy.

days: if Joseph and Mary had really understood the Lord's origin and mission, they would have gone to the Temple first.

Further context. Once again, as in the Presentation, the law is paramount in motivating the events of the narrative. The ancient command to keep the Passover brings the Holy Family to Jerusalem. Exodus 12:2-28 describes the origin of the feast, and Deuteronomy 16:5-6 specifies the place for its observance: "You may not offer the Passover sacrifice within any of your towns which the Lord your God gives you; but at the place which the Lord your God will choose, to make his name dwell in it, there you shall offer the Passover sacrifice, in the evening at the going down of the sun." Hence the trip to Jerusalem; hence also the Lord's last entry into Jerusalem, where he ate the Passover meal with his disciples and instituted the Eucharist on the evening before his crucifixion (Matthew 26, Mark 14, Luke 22). Hence the association of Jesus and the Passover lamb. When Jesus sends his disciples into the city to make arrangements for a place to celebrate the Passover, he is continuing the lifelong habit that we see exemplified in the Finding in the Temple. The importance of the law in the story of the Finding further delineates the character of the Holy Family: of all human families, they were the most aware of the nearness of the Creator and of their obligations to him. Therefore they react to the God-given laws regulating worship and behavior with a compelling sense of duty.

That sense extended to the child Jesus, whose Incarnation brought him fully into the human condition with all its obligations, including obedience to his parents and to God. As a man, he was a member of the chosen people, a people selected by God to bear the divine revelation into the world. This people was held together by the covenant and by the laws that were a part of it. Faith defined the people. Hence the absurdity of some moderns who claim to be both atheists and Jews; those who have renounced the covenant have renounced the principle of their solidarity.

The commandment to honor one's parents occurs in Exodus 20:12—"Honor your father and your mother that your days may be long in the land which the Lord your God gives you"—and is repeated, with slight elaborations, in Deuteronomy 5:16 and elsewhere. Jesus himself repeats the commandment in Matthew 15:4 (parallel to Mark 7:10) and Matthew 19:19 (parallel to Mark 10:19 and Luke 18:20). In the story of the Finding, Jesus shows himself a dutiful child by obeying Joseph and Mary as the law commands. But the law, as Jesus came to show, is not yet perfect. In his role as its "fulfillment,"[37] he shows himself to be behind and above the Torah itself. In doing so, he abrogates parts of the Mosaic law that do not correspond with the natural law; the license to divorce one's wife upon trivial cause, for instance, he attributes to human "hardness of heart" and states that any divorce at all is wrong (Matthew 19:3-12). For the good of marriage is part of God's good creation that existed before the written law—indeed, before writing was invented. Jesus further states that he is "Lord even of the Sabbath" (Mark 2:28). In his ministry he thus affirms his right to supersede "divine positive law," the law that has to come from revelation and not from study or contemplation of nature,[38] and to affirm the law that is at the heart of creation. This law, the divine natural law, preceded all positive law, including that given by God to man. It would seem that obedience to parents is part of this natural law, the law of human nature,[39] which was binding from the beginning of man's creation.

---

[37] Matthew 5:17: "Do not think that I have come to abolish the law and the prophets; I have come not to abolish, but to fulfill them."

[38] See Grisez, *Christian Moral Principles*, p. 278.

[39] See C.S. Lewis, *Mere Christianity* (New York: Macmillan, 1958), pp. 3-25.

Jesus fulfills the obligation to obey to the fullest possible extent. For he renders perfect obedience not only to his Mother and his foster father as he grows up, but to his true Father, the Heavenly Father, throughout his life. He is even quite clear that duly constituted civil authority is to be obeyed; his injunction to "render … to Caesar the things that are Caesar's, and to God the things that are God's" (Matthew 22:21, Mark 12:17, Luke 20:25) clearly teaches that Christians cannot consider themselves exempt from the legitimate requirements of community life. The latter part of the injunction, to obey God, is the principle that brings the Lord to the ultimate sacrifice. It culminates in the Agony in Gethsemane, when he asks in vain to be relieved of his terrible duty but nevertheless expresses his complete acquiescence—his willingness to obey—in the Father's will. The great canticle embedded in St. Paul's letter to the Philippians is the most eloquent direct biblical expression of Christ's obedience: Jesus

> did not consider equality with God something to hold on to. Instead, he emptied himself and took on the form of a slave, born in human likeness, and to all appearances a man. He humbled himself and became obedient even unto death, death on a cross (Philippians 2:6-8).[40]

A further scriptural element in the Finding is its echo of Christ's teaching on the Temple and the body. First, his answer to Mary's question—"Why did you do this to us?"—reflects, in a human sense, his upbringing and, in a divine sense, his origin. He knows that he is the Son of God. He also knows, from twelve years' experience in a devout family, that the Temple is the place where God is to be sought. Hence, "I must concern myself with my

---

[40] Grisez, *Living a Christian Life*, pp. 433-435, gives a thorough discussion of the nature of authority and obedience, including Jesus' own obedience.

Father's affairs." Jesus' knowing that the Temple is God's house says a lot about the relationship of Judaism to Christianity. For instance, it gives the lie to those who say that Christianity is inherently anti-Semitic. We Christians are the inheritors of Judaism. Second, by the time of his public ministry he has nevertheless come to teach that his mission and his capabilities *transcend* the Israelite Temple. He proclaims that "the hour is coming, and is now, when the true worshipers will worship the Father in spirit and truth" (John 4:23), not in Jerusalem. That worship will be oriented toward the Son of Man, who is "Lord even of the Sabbath" (Mark 2:28). Third, as his suffering on Calvary nears, Jesus comes to identify *himself* as the "Temple," indestructible symbol of the New Covenant: "'Destroy this temple, and in three days I will raise it up.' ... [H]e spoke of the temple of his body" (John 2:20-21). Finally, St. Paul draws an analogy between the body of every Christian and the ancient dwelling place of God: "Do you not know that your body is a temple of the Holy Spirit within you, which you have from God? You are not your own; you were bought with a price" (1 Corinthians 6:19-20). So adultery, for instance, is ultimately analogous to desecration of a church.

Extensions and applications. One of the central themes of the Finding is the wisdom of the Lord. "All those listening to him were amazed at his intelligence and his answers," St. Luke writes. "Jesus progressed in wisdom and age and grace before God and men." Pope Leo XIII implies that the Christ Child's wisdom is the chief subject matter of the Finding.[41] It would seem, however, that this wisdom has been largely *concealed* until the Finding, for Mary and Joseph are "amazed." One can imagine Jesus in his earliest years: the perfectly well-behaved, perfectly respectful, perfectly

---

[41] Pope Leo XIII, *Magnae Dei Matris* (On the Rosary), September 8, 1892, no. 30.

humble, honest, trusting, and childlike boy at home with his Mother and foster father. But he has not revealed his inner life, in which constant communion with the Father is the principal feature, either at home or on those annual trips to Jerusalem for the Passover. If he had done so, his parents would not have been astonished at his conversation with the teachers in the Temple. Mary and Joseph's surprise is parallel to their seeking the child all around the city before looking in the Temple. Both reflect an understandable lack of comprehension of the nature and mission of Jesus, whose life continues to unfold surely but still mysteriously before all who see him, particularly his Mother. Although she was the Mother of God, the Blessed Virgin did not share the Lord's divine mind; we may suppose that in her completely human but sinless mind she was often baffled or amazed at her Son's words and deeds. The events that occurred during the years following the Finding, whatever they held, led the Blessed Mother to express her complete faith in the judgment and ability of Jesus at the wedding in Cana.

The nature of wisdom is a major topic of Scripture. In Sacred Tradition, Jesus himself is often identified with the wisdom of God. Those scholars who say that the proverb is the essence of "wisdom literature"[42] are probably right, for a good proverb contains the distilled essence of human experience in a powerful short statement. The book of Proverbs includes many jewels of practical wisdom: "A soft answer turns away wrath, but a harsh word stirs up anger" (Proverbs 15:1); "Like a gold ring in a swine's snout is a beautiful woman without discretion" (11:22). The Lord Jesus, however, uses few if any proverbs of this sort. His utterances that resemble proverbs—chiefly the Beatitudes—far transcend the earthy experience and practical wisdom reflected in the ordinary maxim.

---

[42] See Gerhard von Rad, *Wisdom in Israel* (London: SCM Press, 1972), Chapter 3.

Unlike ordinary proverbs, the Beatitudes are counterintuitive; they state what had never been said and what Jesus' original audience did not expect to hear: "Blessed are the poor in spirit, for theirs is the kingdom of heaven.... Blessed are the meek, for they shall inherit the earth" (Matthew 5:3,5). The Jews did not expect or want a *meek* Messiah. Having believed for centuries in the earthly promise of God's retribution, they could not fathom that the meek should "inherit the earth"; that privilege was for the proud and powerful, whose ownership proved that God was on their side. But the wisdom of the Lord transcended their knowledge and reversed many of their judgments.

The wisdom with which Jesus is associated is not primarily proverbial—or even verbal, except insofar as the Incarnate Word is verbal. At the heart of the mysterious teaching that the Incarnate Word was "spoken" by the Father is the fact that Christ was involved in creating and sustaining all that is. Jesus is the wisdom of God because he was present with the Father at the beginning and because, inseparable from the Father and the Holy Spirit, he was the agent of creation: the wise disposition of the universe in beauty and harmony is often said to be his doing.[43] Christ's wisdom is thus embodied in creation, for creation is a product of God's *mind*; true understanding of the created world therefore leads, even if imperfectly, to a knowledge of God. "The heavens are telling the glory of God; and the firmament proclaims his handiwork" (Psalm 19:1). "The Lord by wisdom founded the earth," says the book of Proverbs in one of its more philosophical passages; "by understanding he established the heavens; by his knowledge the deeps broke forth, and the clouds drop down the dew" (3:19-20).

---

[43] "In the beginning was the Word, and the Word was with God, and the Word was God. He was in the beginning with God; all things were made through him, and without him was not anything made that was made. In him was life, and the life was the light of men. The light shines in the darkness, and the darkness has not overcome it" (John 1:1-5).

Sirach also places wisdom at the origin of creation: "Wisdom was created before all things, and prudent understanding from eternity.... [T]he Lord himself created wisdom; he saw her and apportioned her, he poured her out upon all his works" (Sirach 1:4,9). Because of Catholic teaching on the Holy Trinity, who informed Scripture even before the birth of Christ, the higher wisdom celebrated in Proverbs, Wisdom, Sirach, and many of the Psalms became recognized as the wisdom of Jesus.

And what of the boy in the Temple? If his interlocutors had really understood him, they would have known that his amazing answers could have come only from the Messiah, from "God with us" (Matthew 1:23). The Finding in the Temple records the wisdom of God bursting forth in a new theophany—not in the burning bush of Moses, nor in the voices that came to Ezekiel, but in a preadolescent boy who claims God as his Father.

We still find Jesus in the "Temple," that is, in our churches, where his presence in the tabernacle yet proclaims his origin and divinity. If we visit him there and listen quietly to him, he will impart the wisdom we need to conduct our lives. The wisdom that comes from adoration of the Blessed Sacrament is often wordless, the ineffable witness of the indwelling Spirit. It is often also very practical, for we leave the Presence of his Body with new and precise insights into what God wants us to do. The Bread of Angels can become the wellspring of all our actions.

Joseph and Mary seek and find the Lord, and their joy is amplified by their previous anxiety. This is the last view we get of Jesus until his baptism—the sight of a child sitting among the learned men and surprising them with his wisdom. The scene is enhanced by our knowledge of Christ: we, as his servants and worshipers, know who he is, but the teachers in the Temple don't. What's more, even his Mother is undergoing a demanding learning process. For the moment she may be merely bemused, as she ponders the events of her Son's life. But more, and more painful, surprises are in store for her. These are foreshadowed not only in the Presentation, with Simeon's dark prophecy of a sword that will pierce Mary's soul, but in the unforeseen actions and words of Jesus, which absorb her thought.

Thus the Joyful Mysteries end in ambivalence. They are joyful indeed, but with a final admixture of anxiety and foreboding, of misunderstanding and mystery. The greatest joys are seldom unmixed. Jesus goes back to Nazareth with his Mother and foster father. The obedience that he continues to yield to the Blessed Mother suggests what the Christian attitude toward Mary ought to be. If our Lord so honored her, why should we do less?

Mary's joy at finding Jesus in the Temple. Mary's joy in this mystery is not hard to imagine. What mother would not be joyful at finding a lost son? And yet the Finding introduces a bittersweet element. It adumbrates the separation of Jesus from his Mother—though not, to be sure, a separation through the decline of love, or even much of a physical separation. What it foreshadows is the perilous and ultimately mortal ministry of Christ, whose sacrificial course of life filled his Mother's mind and ultimately pierced her heart with a sword.

Suggested intentions. Jesus astonished his auditors with his wisdom—small wonder, since he is the Wisdom of God incarnate. We should pray that all our thoughts, words, and deeds will embody Christ's wisdom to the greatest extent allowed by our malice, weakness, and ignorance, and that the world may begin to look to the Savior for the guidance it so desperately needs.

Chapter Three

THE SORROWFUL MYSTERIES

The Church celebrates the Passover of Christ
until he returns, "in union with the saints in heaven and
in particular with the Blessed Virgin, whose burning
charity and unshakable faith she imitates."

Pope Paul VI

To contemplate the Sorrowful Mysteries with Mary is to see into the mystery of human life. There are two principal ways of missing the meaning of suffering, which is mysterious by its duality. One is to think of suffering as unmitigated evil, to be abhorred and avoided at all costs. This is the way of the supporters of suicide, of the "nice death" movement. The other is to fail to see the reality of evil in suffering, to shrug it off with the placid assurance that it has no lasting existence in the light of heaven. Both mistakes diminish the significance of suffering. Both degrade the pains of the Incarnate Word, which were mirrored in the heart of his Mother. And both trivialize his injunction to us to take up our crosses and follow him. For suffering can be made holy only when it is accepted. If pain is to be avoided by all means, then so is the cross. If pain is meaningless, then why bother?

Long ago the Holy Father castigated "repugnance to suffering and eagerness to escape whatever is hard or painful to endure." Those who exhibit these traits, he said, "dream of a chimeric civilization in which all that is unpleasant shall be removed, and all that is pleasant shall be supplied."[1] Pope Pius X later used the phrase "law of suffering" to indicate the principle by which Christ liberates the human race from the appalling effects of original sin.[2] Because Mary, conceived without sin, "may be said to have lived the very life of her Son," because of the "community of will and

---

[1] Pope Leo XIII, *Laetitiae Sanctae* (Commending Devotion to the Rosary), September 8, 1893, no. 7.

[2] Pope Pius X, *Ad Diem Illum Laetissimum*, February 2, 1904, no. 22.

suffering between Christ and Mary,"[3] she is a model for the Church. The Church in turn is transformed and saved because it suffers with them. Only by enduring our pains as patiently as possible and offering them to God in union with the pains of Christ can we be saved through his passion. Thus was Mary saved, and the first of the saved.

---

[3] *Ibid.*, nos. 7 and 12.

1

THE AGONY IN THE GARDEN

Littera: Scripture and gloss. In spite of the fact that he knew he would be killed in Jerusalem, Jesus traveled to the city with his disciples to celebrate the Passover. At the meal, which became known as the Last Supper, he instituted the Eucharist in words and actions that are still imitated by his priests at the altar. Subsequently, during the night of Holy Thursday, Jesus underwent great suffering of mind and heart as he looked at his mission and faced his death. With him were the eleven disciples, from whom Judas Iscariot had parted.

> Jesus came with them to a place called Gethsemane, and he said to his disciples, "Sit here, while I go over there and pray." He took Peter and the two sons of Zebedee along and he began to be upset and troubled. Then he said to them, "My soul is greatly distressed, to the point of death; stay here, and stay awake with me." And he went ahead a little and fell face down in prayer, and he said, "My Father, if it is possible, let this cup pass away from me; yet not as I wish, but as you do." When he came to the disciples he found them sleeping, and he said to Peter, "So, you could not stay awake with me for one hour? Stay awake and pray that you won't enter into temptation; for the spirit is willing, but the flesh is weak." He went off a second time and prayed again, saying, "My Father, if it is not possible for this cup to pass without my drinking it, let your will be done." And when he came he again found them sleeping, for their eyes were heavy. So, he left them and

went off again and prayed for the third time, saying the same thing once more. Then he came to the disciples and said to them, "Are you still sleeping and taking your rest? Behold, the hour has arrived and the Son of man will be handed over into the hands of sinners. Get up! Let's be going! See, the one who will hand me over has arrived" (Matthew 26:36-46).

Saint Luke adds that while Jesus was in the garden, "there appeared to him an angel from heaven to strengthen him, and in his anguish he prayed more earnestly; and his sweat became like great drops of blood falling down upon the ground" (Luke 22:43-44).

Only one man in this scene is sweating—the one who is about to suffer torture and death. The others, still ignorant of what is going on, are comparatively cool and so sleepy that they can't stay awake. But there is no need to think of their sleepiness as a moral failing; rather, the scene realistically portrays the difference between a man who is facing death and his associates who are not. Significantly, after they learn better what the kingdom of Christ is about, these men will have no trouble staying awake as *they* face martyrdom. But for now they represent a reality of the human condition: we are all relatively disengaged from the suffering of others, even those whom we love. Such is our human isolation.

Jesus, in great agitation and sorrow, prays to his Father to be relieved of the "cup" that he must drink, and his sweat contains blood. In Scripture when a cup is symbolic, it generally represents experience, usually but not always painful. God says to Jeremiah, for instance, "Take from my hand this cup of the wine of wrath, and make all the nations to whom I send you drink it" (Jeremiah 25:15). Here the cup represents the punishment that comes to those who turn from God to idols. In Psalm 23, perhaps the most famous chapter in all of Scripture, the cup symbolizes God's provident care for his servants: "Thou preparest a table before me in the presence of my enemies; thou anointest my head with oil, my cup overflows." In Gethsemane, the cup represents the pain that the Lord faces as he prepares to complete his mission on earth. As a man, he naturally shrinks from torment and desires to avoid it. His prayer to this effect, uttered three times, is one of several "threes" associated with the Passion—the disciples' three naps, Peter's threefold denial, the three cock-crows, Christ's three days in the tomb.

In the passage about his companions, as in numerous passages in the New Testament, St. Peter is given first mention. This passage, like those others, therefore underlines the primacy of the vicar of Christ, whose leadership of the apostles, even before he is tested and denies the Lord, is thus emphasized. Upon Peter's profession of faith that Jesus is the Messiah, the Lord conferred special authority upon him by giving him the "keys of the kingdom" (Matthew 16:19), a symbolic affirmation of St. Peter's apostolic primacy and authority. Subsequently—for instance, in the book of Acts—his leadership is quite obvious.

Further context. The sons of Zebedee, James and John, have previously requested positions of honor in the kingdom of Christ—the honor of sitting "one at [his] right hand and one at [his] left" (Mark 10:37). Though they are disciples, intimates of the Lord, they don't understand the mission of Jesus or the nature of his kingdom. Confusion about the matter reigns among Christ's followers until the time of the Crucifixion. At the Last Supper, *after* the institution of the Eucharist, "a dispute ... arose among them as to which of them should be considered the greatest" (Luke 22:24)—a clear demonstration of the apostles' lack of understanding. Jesus has taught them, both by his life and words, that greatness in the kingdom comes only through selfless service to others. This is the way, for instance, that the Eucharist becomes the center of the Christian life: it does so precisely to the extent that the individual

Christian's sacrificial life resembles and is joined with the great Sacrifice recapitulated on the altar. James and John had so far learned little from Christ's washing of the apostles' feet. Wanting to be the "greatest" is hardly compatible with obeying the injunction to "wash one another's feet" (John 13:14) in imitation of the Master.

Jesus' emotional state is rarely mentioned in Scripture. Cardinal Newman remarks that even when the Lord must have been joyful or sad, his utterance is marked with a "deep tranquility of mind, which is conspicuous through the solemn history of the Atonement."[4] Rarely do the evangelists say that at a given time he was in a good mood or down in the mouth. Evidently such matters were not important enough to the sacred writers even to be mentioned. The obsession with "having a good day" is a late invention of a culture that puts too much emphasis on "feeling good," an emphasis that is entirely absent from Scripture. Euphoric emotional states were evidently not prized by the inspired authors. Even in the scene that clearly demonstrates the Lord's "righteous anger," for instance—that in which he drives the animal sellers from the Temple (John 2:13-16)—the anger itself is not mentioned. Yet in the Agony passage the Lord's sorrow is so overwhelming that he mentions it *himself*: "[H]e began to be upset and troubled. Then he said to them, 'My soul is greatly distressed, to the point of death'."

Previously, at the death of Lazarus (John 11), we have seen the Lord in great sorrow. He had delayed his visit to Lazarus' household in spite of his friend's mortal illness, and now that Lazarus was dead, Jesus went to Bethany, where Mary, Lazarus' sister, met him. "Lord, if you had been here, my brother would not have died,"

---

[4] John Henry Newman, *Parochial and Plain Sermons* (San Francisco: Ignatius Press, 1987), p. 118.

she said. "When Jesus saw her weeping, and the Jews who had come with her also weeping, he was deeply moved in spirit and troubled; and he said, 'Where have you laid him?' They said to him, 'Lord, come and see.'" And then follows the shortest verse in the Bible, two words in which the great love of God for the human race is comprehended: "Jesus wept." When he went to the tomb, he was again "deeply moved." The Lord, in short, is greatly affected by the death of his friend; in his humanity God is moved by human sorrows and joys. His raising of Lazarus does not overcome the enormity of death, however, for Lazarus dies again. Only the Resurrection brings triumph over the ancient curse. As Jesus faces his own death in Gethsemane, that triumph is a world away, on the other side of the cross. The Lord had resuscitated strangers before he raised Lazarus; as a friend, Lazarus was surely something more to him than a stranger. For the death of a friend has a special effect and a special meaning for oneself: that death comes to all flesh, to my friends and to me. As his friend had died, so must Jesus die if he is to carry out the mission of the Incarnation. But glory was remote—beyond the agony of crucifixion and the gloom of Holy Saturday.

Jesus admonishes St. Peter, "Stay awake and pray that you won't enter into temptation." This advice is directly parallel to the petition in the Lord's Prayer: "lead us not into temptation, but deliver us from evil" (Matthew 6:13; cf. Luke 11:4). The petition is variously interpreted. Some say that it means "Lead us not into too great temptation." Others, mystified by the implied idea that God himself tempts man, think that idea needs reconciling with the goodness of the Creator. The Lord's Prayer speaks in the same terms as much of the Old Testament, where everything that happens is attributed directly to God. The ancient Israelites believed that whatever happened to them was a deserved judgment of God, and yet when in trouble they often believed that they had done nothing to deserve harsh treatment. They therefore protested their innocence and asked God for rectification. The conflict between what one deserves and what one gets receives its fullest treatment in the book of Job—at least up to the ending, which in no way follows from the significance of the rest of the book. By the time of Christ, however, the matter had been long settled: it was clearly recognized that much happens on the earth through secondary causes and is not directly brought about by God. When temptation occurs, it occurs not because God brings it about but because it is a necessary adjunct to the life of man, who is a free moral agent in a world that offers both moral and immoral choices. And yet Jesus uses the language of the psalmists, which figuratively attributes to the Father all that happens, including temptation. The question therefore is stylistic. Jesus knows that temptation doesn't come from the Father, but attributes it to him in a traditional figure of speech: because God *lets* things happen, he is said to cause them. So much for the idea of God as the *agent* of temptation.

The interpretation of "temptation" as "too great temptation" seems mistaken to me. In fact, it runs counter to the inspired teaching of St. Paul: "The only temptations you have received are normal human ones. God is trustworthy and won't allow you to be tested beyond your strength—along with the temptation he will also provide a way out, that you will be able to endure it" (1 Corinthians 10:13). We never encounter a situation that *requires* us to sin, even if doing the right thing is painful. So what does Jesus mean? He means precisely what he says. Because he knows that "the spirit is willing, but the flesh is weak," he tells his disciples to pray that they not be tempted. Period. And, knowing the temptations of the night ahead, he tells St. Peter the same thing. Did Peter obey the admonition and pray not to be tempted? We don't know. But if he did, then his prayer, like that of Christ in the garden, was answered with a negative. Jesus prayed to be spared the cup of suffering, and the Father denied his request. If Peter prayed to avoid temptation, his petition was likewise denied, for he was sorely and effectively tempted to deny Christ. Jesus knows that we give in even to small temptations far too easily, so he advises us to pray that we not be tempted. The effort to shun the occasions of sin is nothing but a morally upright attempt to avoid temptation.

Extensions and applications. Jesus reveals his human heart and soul more directly in the Agony than in any other of the mysteries. In many of the mysteries we must surmise, if we dare, what he is thinking. In the Agony, however, he tells us. He speaks in some mysteries and is silent in others. He speaks in the Finding in the Temple, for instance, but for the purpose of revealing his mission, not for emotional self-revelation. He is silent in the Scourging and on the path to Calvary. When he does speak in other mysteries, he doesn't talk about how he *feels.* Even while he is hanging on the cross, his utterances reflect rather than directly express his love; he does not say "I love you" to his executioners or to the repentant thief, though his prayer and promise (Luke 23:34,43) clearly suggest his love. But in the Agony he speaks directly of his affective state: "My soul is greatly distressed, to the point of death." That speech, plus his bloody sweat and his words to the Father, imprints the Agony indelibly on the Christian consciousness. We consequently see representations of Gethsemane in statues and paintings, in cemeteries and hospital chapels and funeral homes— wherever sorrowful people need reminding that the Lord of heaven and earth was himself subject to agony of spirit. The Agony thus becomes a major symbol of Christ's resemblance to us emotional and sentient human beings.

What are the elements of that symbol? In what respects can we look at Gethsemane and see a reflection of our own lives? Just as Jesus, incarnate as a man, had to undergo essentially all varieties of human suffering, so we, being human, find those varieties in the course of our lives. The details may differ, but in undergoing human pain Christ suffered in basically the same way we do. His suffering is like ours. St. Thérèse writes to a correspondent, "He finds you worthy of suffering for his love, and it is the greatest proof of affection that he may give you, for suffering makes us like him."[5]

Points of resemblance abound. First, Christ is lonely and, practically speaking, deserted in the Agony. Likewise, all other human beings are alone when they face misery or die, no matter how many people are around. In a very real sense, a terminally ill man, though surrounded by relatives and friends, is still alone because he is facing *his* death—something that others cannot do. But Jesus is not only in the situation of facing his Passion and death. His disciples, inevitably less engaged by the coming events than he is, actually desert him by going to sleep, not once but three times. Whenever we feel alone in facing a trial—whether that loneliness comes from an actual lack of companionship or from the sense that no one can really share our load—we should remember that Jesus underwent the same feelings, that he is touched by our plight, that because of him we are really not alone: the Savior is with us. His sufferings are like ours.

The disciples' sleep undoubtedly compounded the Lord's sense of rejection and failure. We don't often think of Jesus as experiencing a sense of failure, but surely such misery is a necessary part of the Agony. He has known other failures. We have already seen him unable to work miracles, for instance, because of the unbelief of the people. When Jesus went to "his own hometown," many people there took offense at him. And "Jesus said to them, 'A prophet is not without honor, except in his own hometown, and among his kinsmen, and in his own house.' And he was unable to do any mighty works there, except that he cured a few sick people by laying his hands on them. And he was astounded at their unbelief" (Mark 6:1,3-6; cf. Matthew 13:57-58).

---

[5]   *Letters of St. Thérèse of Lisieux*, Volume II, trans. John Clarke, O.C.D. (Washington: Institute of Carmelite Studies, 1988), pp. 896-897.

Of course, God's limit upon his own power is entirely voluntary, but it is necessary if man is to have free will. God desires our freely chosen service, for coerced service would be the adulation of puppets, who move only as their strings pull them. God does not want this kind of service. He has no desire to resemble a monarch surrounded by flattering automata. Man was created to "show forth his goodness and to share with us His everlasting happiness in heaven,"[6] and true goodness is never coerced. Therefore God has always given human beings the awesome power of shutting him out. This is what it means to have free will. In the Incarnation, God made it quite clear that he cannot save those who *will* not be saved, for coerced salvation, like coerced love or goodness, is an oxymoron. God sustains all of creation by his love and power; the human rational soul is the only region in which he can be declared off limits. But what a crushing weight of responsibility for our own eternal end comes with that declaration!

In the Agony, Jesus comes to the *human* realization that he has failed to do what he intended. He has taught, he has worked miracles to encourage faith, he has gathered a retinue of disciples, but he has not converted his countrymen, who are now coming to kill him. He knows that his death will be a painful one, and he obviously hopes and prays to escape the suffering of Good Friday. But he is an example to us in his willingness to drink the cup of pain. When human beings deny the value of suffering to the extent that they want to escape it at all costs, they are rejecting the example Christ set. Every person in pain is like Jesus in Gethsemane. Those who seek a painless suicide and thus refuse to bow to the will of God commit the sin of despair. They say, in effect, that suffering is worthless, that it can't be sanctified, that in spite of Jesus

---

[6] *The New Saint Joseph Baltimore Catechism* (New York: Catholic Book Publishing Company, 1964), p. 12.

a painful death cannot be "dignified." This is a major element of the assisted-suicide and euthanasia movements—that they deny the value of suffering. Jesus Christ asks us to do something quite different, however. He asks us to join him in Gethsemane, accept what God sends, and then he enables us to bear it. He assures us that our pains, joined to his, are holy.

Did the man Jesus ever hope to convert the world without dying for it? Did he have, in his human mind, the understandable idea that he might conceivably carry out his mission without the Passion? Such a thought seems to be implied by another famous expression of failure that precedes the Agony: "O Jerusalem, Jerusalem, killing the prophets and stoning those who are sent to you! How often would I have gathered your children together as a hen gathers her brood under her wings, and you would not!" (Matthew 23:37; cf. Luke 13:34). The human will of the Lord is here clearly expressed. Jesus *wanted* something that he was denied—his acceptance as Messiah among the people who looked for the coming of the kingdom. And his will is thwarted—not by his own action, to be sure, but by the freely chosen rejection of the people.

In the Agony we see a Man who has run dead up against the hardness of human hearts that reject him and are now intent upon killing him. When we, with the best will that we can muster in our fallen condition, strive to do good for others—to convert them to Christ, to help them choose a right course of action, to bring out what is best in them, to offer them our good will; when we, with the best of motives, try to enlist the cooperation of others—when we do these things and fail, we are with Christ in Gethsemane. When we see the decay of our culture, as exemplified by the murder of millions of unborn children, by runaway divorce, rampant illegitimacy, by massive and routine violence among fatherless boys, by the cancerous growth of pornography and the widespread acceptance of the homosexual lifestyle, by the promotion of euthanasia, by successful public attacks upon the free practice of religion, we are reminded of the failure of our own efforts to bring about the Culture of Life for which Pope John Paul II is such a strong and hopeful advocate.[7] But if our efforts seem to have failed, we should look to the Lord in Gethsemane. If our prayers have for the moment been answered in the negative, we should look to Jesus in the garden. If we are disappointed that our children, our neighbors, our country have rebelled against the Lord, we should look to Gethsemane, where the failure of our plans and intentions is mirrored in the Son of God. There, Jesus carries all our loneliness, rejection, and failure in his Sacred Heart.

When in his Incarnation God became passible—that is, capable of suffering—the stage was set not only for the Son of Man to skin his knees as a child and have colds and earaches and whatnot, but for the Agony in the Garden. One of the principal features of the Agony is the Lord's quite human dread of pain. When he prays to be spared the cup of suffering, his desire to avoid physical pain is undoubtedly a large part of his motive. He has previously spoken of dying and rising (Matthew 20:17-19, John 2:19), and of the cross as a symbol of endurance and self-sacrifice (e.g., Mark 8:34). He knows what is going to happen after his betrayal. Much of what is encompassed by his prescience on that night is burdensome, humiliating, and dreadfully difficult: the trial, the mockery, the carrying of the cross. But surely it is his foreknowledge of a torturous death that makes him plead to the Father to let him avoid it. As most human beings shrink from pain, Jesus shrank from being nailed to the cross.

The rest of his prayer, that the will of the Father be done, is the culmination of human obedience to the Creator. We can, and indeed must, imitate that obedience by seeking to do the will of

---

[7] See Pope John Paul II's encyclical *Evangelium Vitae* (English version, *Origins*, 24.42 [April 6, 1995]).

the Father rather than our own will, even if it involves suffering. But no matter what suffering is involved, we can never undertake it with the perfect freedom of the sinless Jesus. Because of our sin our own suffering is always in some sense deserved, whereas his was accepted in total freedom. For some sacrifices under the Old Covenant only a spotless lamb or heifer could be used.[8] Under the New Covenant only the sinless Savior could expiate our sins by his death. The bloody sweat of his brow as he accepts the inevitability of his Passion prefigures the water and blood that run from his side when the Roman spear pierces his heart. In his obedience the signs of purity and life blend together in one stream.

A final comment on the Agony. Like the scenes with Lazarus and the Temple merchants, it shows the Lord to be a man of complete emotional honesty. We hear a lot about misdirected emotion, and all of us are more or less guilty of it—that is, of suppressing direct expression of feeling and diverting its energy elsewhere. When a man has a grievance against his employer, for instance, he bawls his wife out and kicks the dog. Of course, a certain amount of restraint or redirection of one's feelings is necessary for keeping the peace, and is not dishonest; if I don't like the food at your house, our relationship will gain nothing by my blatant candor. One can imagine that Jesus always acted with perfect courtesy, even with its indirections. Nevertheless, when the negative emotions of anger and grief assail him, he is direct in their expression. No social stigma tells him that "real men" don't weep. When he is stricken with grief, he cries. When he is overwhelmed with sorrow in the garden, he says so. When he is angry at the profaners of the Temple, he immediately makes a whip and drives them out. The Lord never needed any "assertiveness training."

---

[8]   See, for instance, Numbers 19:2-10 and 28:1-4.

Mary and Gethsemane. The Agony stands as the first of the Sorrowful Mysteries of Our Lady, for in her closeness to Christ she suffered all that he suffered, with a mother's fear and pain added. She must have followed the events of that Thursday night with alarm and dread, as her Son was clearly about to be arrested for capital crimes he hadn't committed. All Jerusalem must have been tense with the news. Could anyone doubt that Mary was informed of the peril in which Jesus stood, or that she was with him in her perturbed spirit?

Suggested intentions. As Jesus neared the culmination of his sacrificial life on earth, his human vulnerability became more and more obvious. Until his birth, the idea that God could be capable of suffering was impossible. We should always keep in mind that at any given moment, countless thousands of human beings are in great pain of body, mind, or spirit. We might offer this decade of the Rosary on their behalf—with a prayer that their sufferings will be sanctified because of Christ's suffering, and that they will find an end of their pain in him.

2

THE SCOURGING

Littera: *Scripture and gloss.* The Scourging of Jesus is mentioned in Matthew, Mark, and John, but only in passing. Luke says nothing of it. St. Matthew's account is typical:

> So when Pilate saw that he was doing no good, but instead a riot was beginning, he took water and washed his hands in full view of the crowd and said, "I am innocent of this man's blood! See to it yourselves!" And in answer the people all said, "His blood be upon us, and upon our children!" Then he released Barabbas to them, but he had Jesus scourged, and he handed him over to be crucified (Matthew 27:24-26).

The evangelists skip over the flagellation of the Lord, it seems, as a transitional or insignificant detail. This fact about the Gospels is a realistic reflection of Pilate's attitude toward the Scourging, for to him it was certainly no big deal. It was done in a perfunctory manner, almost as a minor duty.

Incidentally, the person to be scourged was tied to the top of a low pillar, over which he had to lean so that his back was more or less parallel to the floor. The picture of Christ embracing a pillar to which he is tied is inaccurate. Appropriately enough for his complete humiliation, he had to bow to be whipped.

The exact purpose or function of the Scourging is debatable. Some commentaries say that it was intended to weaken the condemned man preceding crucifixion, so that he would die faster on the cross. If this is Pilate's purpose in scourging Jesus, then the whip is part of the sentence of crucifixion. But St. John records that after the scourging Pilate still sought to release the Lord, a fact which argues that the punishment of crucifixion had not been decided upon. This being the case, it would seem that Pilate was trying to substitute a lesser punishment for the greater one.

What is not debatable is that arrogant men tied the hands of the Son of God and whipped him—a colossal affront to God that would not have occurred if he had not permitted it. One can say this about every aspect of the Passion: God allowed it. Nevertheless, how great was the presumption of the Lord's antagonists—of the Roman procurator (a subordinate provincial governor) Pontius Pilate, of the callous and vulgar soldiers, of the frenzied Jewish leaders.

The completely voluntary nature of the Passion—"a death which he freely accepted," in the words of the Second Eucharistic Prayer—is underscored by the fact that the Lord predicted it, and the Scourging as part of it, at the same time that he predicted the Resurrection. According to St. Mark,

> Now they were on the road, going up to Jerusalem, and Jesus was leading them; and they were amazed, but those following were afraid. Once again he took the twelve and began to tell them the things that were going to happen to him, saying, "Behold, we are going up to Jerusalem; and the Son of man will be handed over to the chief priests and the scribes. They will condemn him to death and hand him over to the Gentiles; they will mock him and spit upon him and scourge him and kill him; and after three days he will rise" (Mark 10:32-34; cf. Matthew 20:17-19, Luke 18:31-32).

In this scene Jesus is freely and voluntarily returning to Jerusalem, where he knows that he will be killed after being scourged.

The release of Barabbas is pivotal to the scourging, for only after Pilate decides to release Barabbas does the obnoxious little functionary know whom to scourge. It is significant that, as St. Luke suggests, Pilate would have scourged Jesus in any case, even if he let him go. Pilate freely admits Jesus' innocence, but states his willingness to "chastise" him anyway before releasing him (Luke 23:16,22). There is no indication that Barabbas was punished, in spite of the fact that he was a known insurrectionist.

Insurrection is Pilate's greatest fear. His capricious, cruel, and extortionate rule of Judea is known to history outside the Gospels.[9] The restiveness of the Jews at the time of the Crucifixion is at least partly a result of Pilate's misrule, which reflected his weakness of character. He fears a riot, and a riot would get him in dutch with his Roman superiors. And so he is willing to give the people—or at least the loud ones, "the chief priests and the Pharisees" (John 11:47), whose hostility to Jesus brings on the incident—what they want. For their part, the accusers blame Jesus for the unrest in Judea, but only for the purpose of getting him killed; they know their charges are false. The accusers argue before Pilate that Jesus "is inciting the people, teaching throughout all of Judea, starting from Galilee as far as here" (Luke 23:5). But it is really the Jewish leaders who are stirred up, with an agitation that results almost exclusively from envy of Christ's miracles and fear at the fact that the Lord has gained a large following. Thus they suggest that Jesus is a threat to Rome, and in doing so cynically violate the commandment not to bear false witness (Exodus 20:16). The opposition to

---

[9] The fourth-century Church historian Eusebius, for instance, quotes the first-century philosopher Philo Judaeus to the effect that Pilate looted the sacred treasure of the Jews to build an aqueduct, after which he had the protesters against this act of pilferage clubbed to death. (Eusebius, *Ecclesiastical History*, trans. Kirsopp Lake and J.E.L. Oulton [Loeb Classical Library, Cambridge, Massachusetts: Harvard University Press, 1926, 1932], pp. 123f.)

Jesus is a gang of religious leaders who are upset with him on religious and not political grounds, but who cynically use politics to rid themselves of this upstart prophet, whom they hate and envy. The last thing they will admit is the obvious conclusion to which Christ's miracles point: that he is the Messiah. Therefore, in their zeal to maintain their own standing and their hardhearted inability to modify their preconceived and mistaken notion of the Messiah, they have taken literally Caiaphas' suggestion about how to restore order in Judea.

The matter is recorded in the Gospel of St. John. Certain Jews who had not accepted Jesus as the Messiah nevertheless were impressed by the miracles he performed and the converts he was making. They feared that if the Jewish people at large became his followers, the Romans would smell an insurrection and destroy the nation in a preemptive attack. Caiaphas knows how the Romans will react to a provincial insurrection, so he offers the priests and Pharisees a way to get rid of the noxious Jesus and at the same time to defuse the political danger: "Caiaphas, who was the high priest that year, said to them, 'You don't know anything! Don't you realize that it is better for one man to die for the people than to have the whole nation destroyed?'" (John 11:50). Later, when Jesus was arrested, "they led him first to Annas—he was the father-in-law of Caiaphas" (John 18:14).

How long had these two sought for a Jew who might be sacrificed in order to appease Rome? In the context of Caiaphas' Machiavellian suggestion, the release of Barabbas becomes almost unbearably ironic. Barabbas would, we must assume, have done what Caiaphas wanted: Barabbas was *in fact* an insurrectionist, as Jesus was not. His death would have averted the destruction of the nation. The Jewish leaders at the trial of Jesus could just as well have called for the execution of Barabbas. But because of their hardhearted envy and fear they falsely accused Christ of insurrection and demanded his death.

That death indeed brought about the salvation of the "nation," though not in the way foreseen by Caiaphas. The Temple, symbol of Jewish identity, was destroyed a few years later. The Jewish nation was not saved as a political entity. The death of Jesus, however, brought salvation to the City of God in the whole human race, the "nation" that comprises the beneficiaries of his Passion. St. John points out this dramatic irony in Caiaphas' suggestion. In recommending that one man die to prevent destruction of the nation, Caiaphas, according to St. John, was willy-nilly prophesying the universal salvific gift of the death of Jesus, though the fact was unknown to the high priest. John says that Caiaphas did not make his suggestion "on his own, but since he was high priest that year he prophesied that Jesus would die for the nation, and not only for the nation, but also so that the scattered children of God might gather into one" (John 11:51-52). Caiaphas is a salient example of how Providence works: since the Fall of man, which ultimately brought forth untold good, God has made grace spring forth even from the cynical deeds of perverse men.

Further context. I wish further to illuminate ways in which the Scourging echoes passages from the Old Testament and becomes part of Christian thinking about the Savior. On the one hand it represents the humiliation and pain of Christ, and on the other, the healing of the human race. Furthermore, those who suffer for their faith in Christ are paradoxically healed by their own wounds because of him.

Flogging, according to Scripture, has its moral uses. "Blows that wound cleanse away evil; strokes make clean the innermost parts" (Proverbs 20:30). Deserved punishment, humbly received, is sanative. Deuteronomy 25:1-3 describes the judicial procedure for scourging in the Mosaic law:

> If there is a dispute between men, and they come into court, and the judges decide between them, acquitting the

> innocent and condemning the guilty, then if the guilty
> man deserves to be beaten, the judge shall cause him to
> lie down and be beaten in his presence with a number of
> stripes in proportion to his offense. Forty stripes may be
> given him, but not more; lest, if one should go on to beat
> him with more stripes than these, your brother be degraded
> in your sight.

Certainly, as the testimony of the later Jewish custom of limiting the stripes to thirty-nine suggests, more than forty lashes would suggest contempt for the offender's life; and that is degradation. Some Jewish scholars have maintained that in ancient Jewish society scourging, a normal punishment for infractions, was applied to commoner, priest, and king alike, and that it carried no onus of humiliation. Surely when the scourging takes place in the presence of a judge and the accuser only, as in the passage from Deuteronomy, the humiliation is somewhat limited. But it is hard to imagine that public whipping is ever anything besides humiliating. It might be true that a troublesome schoolboy, for instance, could develop a certain devil-may-care bravado in the course of repeated punishments so that he refused in front of his peers to *appear* humiliated, but that fact doesn't erase the intrinsic ignominy of such punishment.

Although Pilate may have put scourging forward as a lesser punishment for Jesus or as a perfunctory prelude to crucifixion, disgrace remained in the process itself, which consisted of being stripped to the waist, strapped to a pillar, and whipped in the presence of jeering soldiers. At the very least, the Scourging of the Lord represents a violent, if oblique, rejection of the Messiah and his message. But when seen in the broad context of Scripture it represents much more besides. Not only that, but its additional meanings were evidently on the Lord's mind as he faced it. Jesus makes the significance of his Passion as a whole clear by his applications of Scripture to himself; his quotation on the cross, for instance, of

Psalm 22:1—"My God, my God, why have you forsaken me?"—clearly indicates that he allies himself with the forlorn speaker of that psalm. Jesus thus identifies himself with outcasts, rejected people who are degraded socially. Further, in the Gospel quoted above, on the way to Jerusalem he mentions his own flagellation in the context of mockery and spitting. These are universal signs of contempt, and those who bear them are universally humiliated. The Scourging of the Lord, in his own clear concept of it, is an ingredient in the degrading treatment of a human scapegoat-sacrifice, a man who becomes an object of scorn, ridicule, and public debasement. Flogging, the book of Proverbs states, is "for the backs of fools" (Proverbs 19:29). As such, the act is certainly directed toward humiliating the victim.

In addition to legal punishment, the other principal idea associated with scourging is that of slavery. This is true both in Scripture and in broader human history. In American history, for instance, flogging was an especially degrading kind of punishment routinely administered to slaves. Generally, slave owners and freemen of all sorts who had violated the law got more dignified punishments, whereas slaves were subject to whipping at the discretion of their owners—without any trial, and for almost any kind of disobedience. The scriptural record bears out the analogy between black American and Jewish slaves. "One day, when Moses had grown up, he went out to his people and looked on their burdens; and he saw an Egyptian beating a Hebrew, one of his people. He looked this way and that, and seeing no one he killed the Egyptian and hid him in the sand" (Exodus 2:11-12). Thus Moses, in the first awakening of his vocation to lead his people to freedom, avenges the routine treatment of a Hebrew slave. Scourging is for human chattels, not for the free.

The class and political associations of scourging are nowhere clearer than in the account of St. Paul's judicial appeal to Rome. Paul recounts his conversion and asserts to his fellow Jews that Jesus has sent him to the Gentiles. This "ecumenical" opening of the Kingdom to non-Jews is inflammatory:

> Up to that point the crowd had listened to him; but then they raised their voices and said, "Away from the earth with such a man! He's not fit to live." And as they shouted and waved their cloaks and threw dust into the air, the tribune ordered Paul to be brought into the barracks, and ordered him to be interrogated under the whip to find out the reason they were shouting at him like that. But when they had tied him up with thongs, Paul said to the centurion who was standing by, "Are you allowed to scourge a Roman citizen without a trial?" When the centurion heard this, he went to the tribune and said, "What are you doing? This man is a Roman!" So the tribune came and said to him, "Tell me, are you a Roman citizen?" "Yes," he said. The tribune answered, "I paid a lot of money for my citizenship." And Paul said, "But I am a citizen by birth." At once, the men who had been about to interrogate him stepped back; the tribune also was frightened when he realized that Paul was a Roman citizen and that he had him bound (Acts 22:22-29).

Rank has its privileges. If St. Paul hadn't been a Roman citizen, he could have been "examined" by beating until the soldiers heard what they thought was the truth. In the same situation the ordinary Judaean, legally inferior to the ordinary Roman, would have been whipped like a slave. Like Jesus.

In its general intent and function, therefore, the Scourging was a process for humiliating the Lord. But attacks on God and his Anointed backfire eternally and paradoxically, not only in Scripture but in history, for the wounds of Christ bring healing. The Suffering Servant of Isaiah "was wounded for our transgressions ... bruised for our iniquities; upon him was the chastisement that made us whole, and with his stripes we are healed" (Isaiah

53:5). St. Peter writes of Jesus, "It was he who bore our sins in his body on the cross so that we could die to sin and live in righteousness; by his wounds you have been healed" (1 Peter 2:24).

Extensions and applications. The meaning of the Scourging is extended further in Scripture and Tradition. At Catholic altars the Church offers the perfect sacrifice, the body and blood of Jesus. Because the members of the Church are able to offer themselves to the Father at the same altars, their sacrifices resemble that of Christ and become meritorious because of his sacrificial suffering and death. The Church is therefore a "kingdom of priests"— not of ordained priests but of individuals whose sacrifices are acceptable to the Creator. For this reason, when the people of God are themselves scourged, their stripes become an offering to the Lord through which they are healed. The saints *accept* their stripes in imitation of Christ and are thereby healed. We are healed not only by Christ's stripes but, because of him, by our own.

The author of the book of Hebrews reflects on how past people of faith "drew strength from weakness.... Some were tortured but refused to accept release that they might rise again to a better life. Others were mocked and scourged, put in chains and imprisoned" (Hebrews 11:34-36). Paul and Silas were similarly treated: "The crowd joined in the attack on them; and the magistrates tore the robes off Paul and Silas and ordered that they be beaten with rods. After administering a severe beating to them, they threw them into prison" (Acts 16:22-23). Jesus had prophesied as much: "Beware of men; they will hand you over to councils, and scourge you in their synagogues, and you will be led before governors and kings for my sake, as a witness to them and to the Gentiles" (Matthew 10:17-18). St. Paul reflects on his own experiences of scourging: "Five times I received forty lashes less one from the Jews" (2 Corinthians 11:24); "as servants of God," he writes, "we commend ourselves in every way possible with great steadfastness—in afflictions, in dire need, in distress, when beaten, in prison, subjected to mob violence, in hard work, in sleepless nights, in fasting…" (2 Corinthians 6:4-5). St. Paul and his missionary companions are an embodiment of the Beatitudes:

> Blessed are those who are persecuted for doing God's will, for theirs is the kingdom of heaven.
> Blessed are you when they insult you and persecute you and say every sort of evil thing against you because of me. Rejoice and be glad because your reward will be great in heaven—they persecuted the prophets before you in the same way (Matthew 5:10-11).

Jesus calls us to be similar exemplars of his Beatitudes. When we are discriminated against or ridiculed because of him, our metaphorical stripes become a means of blessing to us. This ridicule is never far away. But we who believe in his word and act accordingly should quietly rejoice that we are counted worthy to suffer that scorn. In various parts of the world, hostility to Christ is more violent; in China, for instance, bishops, priests, and ordinary Catholics are routinely imprisoned for their loyalty to the Church. They bear real stripes, by which they are greatly and fearfully blessed.

Mary and the Scourging. Mary's suffering continued to be vicarious but intense. She knew all about the customary treatment of accused criminals in the Roman court. To see her Son beaten like an unsatisfactory slave must have seemed the negation of that triumph about which she sang in the Magnificat: "He has pulled down the mighty from their thrones, and exalted the lowly" (Luke 1:52). The triumph of darkness over light and innocence must have appeared absolute.

Suggested intentions. The ultimate goal of Christ's sacrifice is to deliver us from bondage to sin and death. He became man "so that through his death he would destroy the one who has power over death, that is, the Devil, and in this way would deliver those who all their lives were in bondage through fear of death" (Hebrews 2:14-15). In order to liberate us from slavery, he took upon himself the nature of a slave, of which being whipped is a prime property. In thanksgiving for the freedom that he won us, let us remember the Scourging and ask the Lord to help us use our freedom in his service.

3

THE CROWNING WITH THORNS

Littera: Scripture and gloss. Matthew, Mark, and John give accounts of the Crowning with Thorns. Here is St. Matthew's version: immediately after the Scourging,

> Then the governor's soldiers took Jesus along to the praetorium, and they gathered the whole cohort around him. They stripped him and put a scarlet robe on him, and after weaving a crown of thorns they put it on his head and a reed in his right hand. And they knelt before him and mocked him, saying, "Hail, King of the Jews!" And after spitting on him, they would take the reed and beat him over the head. And when they had mocked him, they stripped the robe off him and dressed him in his own clothes and led him off to be crucified (Matthew 27:27-31).

St. Mark's version (Mark 15:16-20) is virtually identical. St. John, however, adds important details and incidents. According to John, after Jesus is crowned with thorns and robed in purple, Pilate presents him to the crowd in that array:

> Pilate went outside again, and said to them, "Look, I am bringing him out to you so that you will know that I find no case against him." So Jesus came outside, wearing the crown of thorns and the purple robe. And Pilate said to them, "Look at the man!" When they saw him, the chief priests and their attendants cried out and said, "Crucify him, crucify him!" (John 19:4-6).

Then, after further questioning of Jesus inside the praetorium, Pilate took Jesus out again and sat down on the judgment seat.

> He said to the Jews, "Here is your king!" They shouted, "Away with him, away with him, crucify him!" Pilate said to them, "Shall I crucify your king?" The chief priests answered, "We have no king but Caesar" (John 19:14-15).

The Crowning with Thorns comes at the center of the Rosary and is centered, though obliquely, on the genuine kingship of Christ, whose reign should be the central feature of our lives. The robe, the scepter, the crown, the kneeling and hailing: all are elements of a play-acted scene mocking a royal court. Although nothing in the episode lacks irony, two elements stand out as colossally ironic: (1) The soldiers, ignorant of the reality of Christ's true kingship, think that they are mocking a pseudo-king but are really ridiculing their own Creator. (2) The chief priests are speaking with arch hypocrisy: they would be delighted to have a king besides Caesar, if he was the kind of king who would run the Romans out of the Promised Land and set up a glorious, independent Jewish kingdom. And yet their lie expresses a willingness to do anything required, to profess any allegiance, as long as it will get rid of this troublesome Jesus. Thus their mendacious acknowledgment of "no king but Caesar" is a genuine rejection of their true King.

Further context. In the Gospels, Jesus himself claims kingship only indirectly. Pilate asks him, "Are you the king of the Jews?" and Jesus responds, "You say so" (Luke 23:3). This answer, we are told, amounts to an understated affirmative. But elsewhere in Scripture and throughout the Christian tradition, proclamations of the kingly role of Jesus are much more direct. The great Ambrosian Hymn *Te Deum* calls Christ the "Rex Gloriae," the "King of Glory." We have seen above, in the discussion of the Annunciation, how

St. Luke applied Old Testament prophecies of a messianic king in the line of David to Jesus. We will see below, in the Coronation, how the queenship of Mary accords with Christ's kingship. At the Nativity, St. Matthew records how wise men from the East, led by a star, traveled to Bethlehem seeking the one "who has been born king of the Jews" (Matthew 2:2). The Church proclaims Jesus the universal King on the last Sunday of the Church year, the solemnity of Christ the King. "Crown him with many crowns," the congregation sings.

The Crowning with Thorns is a mockery of a coronation, however; it brings pain and ridicule, not honor, and it does so specifically by parodying a royal ceremony. More than mere rejection, it thus epitomizes the various renunciations of Jesus and his teaching found in the New Testament. Although the Gospels record the Lord's notable successes in gaining followers, they also record notable rejections. We have seen, for instance, how when he went to "his own hometown" and taught in the synagogue, his audience asked in astonishment,

> "Where did this man get this wisdom and these mighty works? Is not this the carpenter's son? Is not his mother called Mary? ... Where did he get all this? And they rejected him. But Jesus said to them, "A prophet is without honor only in his own hometown and in his own house." And because of their unbelief he did not do many mighty works there (Matthew 13:53-55, 56-58).

Then again, his wonderful teaching on himself as the Bread of Life (in John 6) caused many of his followers to take offense and turn away from him. This particular defection was replayed on a grand scale in the Protestant Reformation, when whole nations rejected the teaching of St. John and the Church on transubstantiation. These scriptural renunciations of Jesus culminate in the events of the Passion that we call the Sorrowful Mysteries.

Extensions and applications. Of all the mysteries of the Rosary, none is more full of ironies than the Crowning with Thorns. What a genius of cruelty and derision—indeed, what a great practical joker—was the soldier who devised the crown. He was probably always the life of the party. You can almost hear him: "The revolutionary from Nazareth is supposedly the 'king of the Jews,' so let's crown him!" And then, amid their laughter at such a witty stroke, he tells his companions his idea, and they fashion a crown (actually a kind of cap) of thorns.

The crown itself appears in Christian iconography as one of the "instruments of the Passion," along with the nails, the scourge, the spear, the cross, and other elements. In the Middle Ages these emblems were used as starting points for meditation on Christ's suffering.

It would be hard to imagine a more powerful composite symbol of ridicule, rejection, and cruelty than that crown. Its resemblance to a real crown mocks Jesus, and the thorns pierce his head as the soldiers whack it down with the reed; the reed itself is a rustic parody of a scepter. The crown also suggests a parody of the laurel wreath that was a typical Roman sign of honor. I have read foolish modern comments on the Crowning claiming that the soldiers intended no pain. But surely other materials for a mock crown were abundant—sticks, thornless plants, rope, cord, wood, feathers. Many things could have been used but were not. It was certainly no accident that the soldiers' choice fell upon a plant with thorns that would penetrate to the skull and cause great pain.

And yet we see them acting ignorantly. This is the essence of what is called "dramatic irony": an audience or observer knows something vital that is unknown to the actors in the drama, who are behaving to their own detriment. We know, as the Roman soldiers did not, that he whom they crowned and mocked is indeed the King of the universe, the King of kings. They mocked him because they thought he was a little provincial pipsqueak who needed to be squashed in the interest of public order, and also because they had an all-too-human cruel streak that he offered them an opportunity to employ. The Jewish leaders wanted him executed because they, expecting a different kind of king, thought he was an imposter and blasphemer.

But we as Christians know from the life and teaching of Christ what kind of king he was and what his example means to us. Jesus didn't come into the world to be an ordinary king, but to show his followers the spiritual and moral realities of a kingdom that is "not of this world" (John 18:36). It had always been a feature of the king of Israel that his power was not absolute, but dependent upon God. As the psalmist sings, "our shield belongs to the Lord, our king, to the Holy One of Israel" (Psalm 89:18). In contrast to ancient Egypt, where kings were thought to be divine, in Israel there is no question of self-sufficiency or omnicompetence on the part of the ruler. The king, the "shield," *belongs* to God. But the Jewish leaders who had Jesus crucified nevertheless expected a ruler who would be strong in an earthly, physical way. They had no concept of what constitutes real power. Jesus' reign is radically different from what they expected, for it embodies not a different "leadership style" but the proposition that humility, spiritual poverty, mutual forbearance, self-sacrifice—all the manifestations of love of God and neighbor—were the path to blessedness. "When I am weak, then I am strong," St. Paul wrote (2 Corinthians 12:10).

Jesus allies his kingdom not with the earthly trappings of rulership, but with self-abnegation and servitude: "The Son of man … came not to be served but to serve, and to give his life as a ransom for many" (Mark 10:45). This is also the model for Christ's followers, who, like their Lord, "are not of the world" (John 17:14). In the dynamics of *his* kingdom, greatness comes only through service and self-effacement, not through self-preening and self-congratulation. "He who is greatest among you," Christ said, "shall be your servant; whoever exalts himself will be humbled, and whoever humbles himself will be exalted" (Matthew 23:11-12; cf. Mark 10:43-44). This is what the Blessed Virgin sang about at the Visitation.

One of the most important lessons to learn from the Crowning with Thorns is the nature of the accolades *we* should expect from the world. Our Lord worked miracles and spoke with unmatched wisdom, yet the only sort of applause given him in his final trial was ridicule and pain. As we have seen, he promised his disciples that they would follow in his footsteps—that they would be imprisoned, scourged like him, laughed to scorn, sometimes even killed. Jesus never promised—and never received—high honor from worldly authorities. Instead, he was crowned with thorns and killed to satisfy the rage of a mob. We should expect no greater crown than the one he wore. When we are honored we should be a bit uneasy lest we start thinking in our pride that without God's help we have *earned* the accolades we get. Success in human endeavor comes from God alone: "Our help is in the name of the Lord, who made heaven and earth" (Psalm 124:8), not in our own competence. A Catholic should always be at least somewhat suspicious of civil honors, honorary degrees, or high position. He should remember that Jesus received none of these and nothing like any of them, but that he was crowned with ridicule and pain.

We should consider it an honor to wear a similar crown. "Blessed are you," Jesus said on the mountain, "when men insult you and persecute you and say every sort of evil thing against you falsely because of me. Rejoice and be glad because your reward will be great in heaven—they persecuted the prophets before you in the same way" (Matthew 5:11-12).

Mary and the Crowning with Thorns. There are two coronations in the mysteries of the Rosary. The first gives shame and pain to the King of Heaven, and the second gives glory and honor to his Mother, the Queen of Heaven. Mary's heart was crowned with pain when Jesus was crowned with thorns. If, like her, we are willing to wear the crown that Christ wore on the earth, like her we will be crowned in heaven.

Suggested intentions. Jesus, the King of Heaven and Earth, was crowned on earth with mockery and pain. Let us pray that in every aspect of our lives he will always be crowned with glory and honor, and that all mankind will acknowledge his true reign. For Christians, this is what "thy kingdom come" has to mean.

4

THE CARRYING OF THE CROSS

Littera: Scripture and gloss. St. John's is the only Gospel account of Jesus' carrying his own cross: "So they took Jesus in charge. And carrying the cross himself, he went out to what was called 'the Place of the Skull,' in Hebrew *Golgotha*" (John 19:17).

The other evangelists mention only Simon of Cyrene as the bearer of the cross. The record of St. Mark is the most circumstantial: "they forced a passerby, one Simon of Cyrene, the father of Alexander and Rufus, who was coming in from the country, to take up his cross. And they brought him to the place called *Golgotha*, which, translated, is 'the Place of the Skull'" (Mark 15:21-22). We know no more from Scripture about Simon.

Evidently Jesus carried the cross at the beginning of the trek and, when he became unable through exhaustion to go farther, was relieved of it by Simon. The part of the cross that was usually carried was the cross-beam, not the entire cross. The upright part was usually stationary. Nevertheless, the whole cross is represented in virtually all Christian art that depicts the Carrying; it is at the conceptual center of the Christian memory of the Passion. In the Roman Empire, crucifixion was the customary punishment for the vilest criminals and the lowest social ranks. Roman citizens were not crucified. Jesus, a member of a subject race accused of sedition, though expressly pronounced innocent by his judge, was given the punishment he would have received if he had been guilty. Then, to add to his degradation, he was forced to carry the instrument of his own execution to the place of his death. His way from the Praetorium to Golgotha is called the Via Crucis, the Way of the Cross.

Further context. The entire Passion must be viewed in the context of Christ's popular triumph, which so alarmed the Jewish leaders. Just a few days before his arrest and trial, the Lord had entered Jerusalem to shouts of praise, while the crowd spread branches and garments on his path. The crowd was not, of course, composed of religious leaders, most of whom opposed Jesus. It was made up of his followers, generally humble people, who had seen his miraculous works and listened to his teaching. Happily lacking an ax to grind, they saw the Lord's ministry as a promise of beatitude; but they expressed their expectation in terms that fanned the fires of jealousy among the priests, scribes, and Pharisees. As Jesus rode into the city, "Hosanna!" called the crowd, "Blessed is he who comes in the name of the Lord! Blessed is the coming kingdom of our father David! Hosanna in the highest!" (Mark 11:9-10). Just what kind of kingdom they expected cannot be clearly ascertained; it may have been very much like the kingdom desired by the leaders. But it is certain that the worshiping crowd, in contrast to the chief priests, believed Jesus was the one to bring it. In hailing him as a king like David, however—just as the angel had done at the Annunciation—they provided the envious leaders with ammunition for the charge of sedition.

Just where was the Palm Sunday crowd while Jesus walked the Via Crucis? Some of them were still around, following from a distance but cowed by the military presence. Fear of the Romans would have prevented them from interfering. There is a good chance that others of them had been won over by the chief priests' condemnation of Jesus and now opposed him. Also, many of them must have thought that they had been wrong in acclaiming Jesus as the Davidic king—after all, he had been tried and sentenced without offering any kind of physical resistance or effective verbal defense. Could that have happened to King David's heir? It seems certain that no one in the crowd, including the apostles (wherever most of them were), had a clear idea of the shining victory that the Lord was about to win. They could not come to an understanding of the Resurrection before the event itself. Many Christians have attributed to biblical figures a theological understanding of future matters that they could not have had. To the apostles (not to mention the prophets, or sometimes even Adam) has been attributed anachronistic knowledge that could have come only from the teaching of ecumenical councils of the Church. But we may be sure that, except for some vague hope that their trust in the Lord would not be disappointed, the apostles themselves, and the crowds that followed the Lord, were as discouraged and baffled as anyone else by his Passion. This set the stage, of course, for the glorious surprise they had when Jesus walked again among them.

The Stations of the Cross is an honored traditional devotion based on an imaginative version of what happened as Jesus trod the path to Golgotha. It probably originated as a way of making the Way of the Cross vivid for devotees who were unable to go to Jerusalem on a pilgrimage. It was popular in the Middle Ages. The "stations" are visual images, usually pictures (Westminster Cathedral in London has sculptures by Eric Gill), that represent incidents on the way. They are usually arranged in sequence along the nave of a church. At each station the worshipers stop, meditate, and pray; between the stations they often sing a stanza of a hymn. Although it is a good practice to "make" the Stations of the Cross at any time, the customary time for public observance of the devotion is Lent, especially Fridays, and the Easter Triduum, especially Good Friday. The subject itself is, to be sure, scriptural. But the number and nature of the stations, which recall traditional events that occurred on the Via Crucis, has varied considerably. The modern form of fourteen stations, or stopping places, was not fixed until the eighteenth or nineteenth century.

The Stations of the Cross are: (1) Christ is condemned to death; (2) he carries his cross; (3) he falls the first time; (4) he meets his Mother; (5) Simon of Cyrene is compelled to carry the cross;

(6) St. Veronica wipes the face of Jesus; (7) Christ falls again; (8) he meets the women of Jerusalem; (9) he falls a third time; (10) his garments are taken; (11) he is nailed to the cross; (12) he dies on the cross; (13) his body is taken down; (14) he is laid in the tomb.

The stations focus on Jesus and the cross, and their meaning is generally clear enough. The "women of Jerusalem" whom he meets after Simon has been introduced appear in St. Luke's Gospel:

> Now a large crowd of the people was following him, as well as women who were lamenting and wailing him. But Jesus turned to them and said, "Daughters of Jerusalem, do not weep for me, but weep instead for yourselves and for your children, because, behold the days are coming in which they will say, 'Blessed are those who are barren, and the wombs that never gave birth, and the breasts that did not nurse!' Then they will say to the mountains, 'Fall on us!' and to the hills, 'Cover us!' Because if they do these things when the wood is green, what will happen when it is dry?" (Luke 23:27-31).

The women include the Galileans who followed the Lord when he went to Jerusalem for the last time, as well as other Jewish women who turn out to console Jewish prisoners condemned by the Romans. Although the precise meaning of the evidently proverbial green and dry wood is obscure, one may safely say that the Lord is looking forward to times that will be worse for the women he is addressing. If things like this happen when times are relatively flourishing (in a "green tree"), he suggests, then what will happen when they have deteriorated? The *Oxford English Dictionary* glosses the term "green tree" as "under conditions not involving pressure or hardship." The clear meaning is that pressure and hardship are coming soon—a prophecy quickly fulfilled for the Jewish people and the Church.

Women are also mentioned by St. Mark as being present after the Crucifixion:

> There were also women there watching from a distance, among them Mary Magdalene and Mary the mother of James the younger and of Joses, and Salome—they had followed him when he was in Galilee and served him— and many other women who had come up with him to Jerusalem (Mark 15:40-41).

In addition to Jesus' relation with the Blessed Mother, much could be said about his relations with women. Radical feminists falsely claim that women in Western society have usually been treated as mere property; but it is certain that Jesus didn't treat them so, and they have never been treated so where the teachings of Christ were truly observed. (Exceptions occur, but who can account for every case? Even today, Christian women and children are sold into slavery in southern Sudan, for instance.) The Scriptures give accounts of a number of strong, independent, and influential women—without, however, attacking the goodness of God's creation by pretending that men and women are or ought to be the same, or that they cannot have different roles in the kingdom of God.

The Blessed Virgin appears in only one incident of the Stations, that commemorated by the fourth station, in which Jesus meets his Mother. That meeting, however, is sufficient to impress upon our minds the sad and fearful eyes of Mary as she sees her son carrying his cross toward his execution. Our Lady of Sorrows is here already in her deepest sorrow. Our eyes focus on that encounter, the meeting of eyes between the Son and the Virgin Mother—a meeting of unspeakable grief and pain on both sides.

This pain was undertaken, like all of the Passion, for the salvation of a race defective in its will, scarred, dulled, and mentally unbalanced by sin, purblind and ignorant of its own good—a fallen race that cannot perfect itself or even improve without help. One of the sinful human traits embodied in the story of the Carrying of the Cross is indifference to the suffering of others. I have spoken of the radical alteration in the Jewish crowd between the Triumphal Entry into Jerusalem and the journey to Golgotha—a transformation from cheering unanimity to shrinking fragmentation. Part of that alteration is surely a result of indifference. Just as the apostles, not being themselves threatened by death (yet), went to sleep in the Garden of Gethsemane, so the cowering and absence of Christ's followers as he walked to his death must have been due at least in part to the sentiment "Better him than me, let's get back to routine." Now that he whom they had accepted as Messiah had failed to usher in the kind of kingdom they sought, they had to get on with their lives, and so they shrugged and went about their business. W.H. Auden's poem "Musée de Beaux Arts" is a quiet little masterpiece on this subject. It muses that suffering occurs "While someone else is eating or opening a window or just walking dully along"; "even the dreadful martyrdom must run its course/ Anyhow in a corner, some untidy spot/ Where the dogs go on with their doggy life and the torturer's horse/ Scratches its innocent behind on a tree."[10]

Extensions and applications. In one of the most powerful passages of the Gospels, our Lord meets a rich young man who asked what he must do to receive eternal life. Jesus answered that he must keep the commandments given to Moses. The inquirer stated that he was in the habit of doing so; and then he asked, "What else do I need to do?"

> Jesus said to him, "If you want to be perfect, go, sell your
> possessions and give to the poor, and you will have treasure
> in heaven; and come, follow me." Now when the young

---

[10] W.H. Auden, "Musée de Beaux Arts," *The Collected Poetry of W.H. Auden* (New York: Random House, 1945), p. 3.

man heard this he went away sad, because he had many properties (Matthew 19:16-20).

Elsewhere the Lord says to a crowd of listeners, "If anyone would come after me, let him deny himself and take up his cross and follow me" (Mark 8:34; cf. Luke 9:23).

Just what was the cross that the rich young man was enjoined to take up? It was precisely the renunciation of that which made him what he was, a *rich* young man. It was the habit of a lifetime, in which he could see no evil. He was content enough to abstain from the sins of adultery, murder, lying, and so forth, but the Lord asked this further step of him, which he would not take. His life was invested in his riches, instead of the other way around, and they came paradoxically to own and control him.

Just what is the cross that Jesus asks *us* to take up? We may never know, without a great deal of rigorously honest self-examination, for the renunciation that the Lord requires of us is very often just like that required of the young man: we may be called upon to renounce something (or somebody) to which our souls are so habituated that we are unaware of our slavery.[11] That in which we are so deeply imbued that we are unaware of it may be the very object of our required self-denial. Self-blindness, often self-induced, keeps us from seeing the biggest impediments to our spiritual growth. Usually when we hear the injunction to "take up your cross," we think in melodramatic terms of something that will probably never happen—a demand to undergo extreme persecution or even suffer martyrdom for the sake of Christ. We see ourselves tied to a stake, undergoing heroic and dramatic immolation while the enemies of Christ pile wood on the fire. But the fact is that usually the crosses we are called to bear are much more subtle—indeed,

---

[11] Cf. C.S. Lewis, "The Trouble with X," *God in the Dock*, ed. Walter Hooper (Grand Rapids: Eerdmans Publishing Company, 1970), pp. 151-155.

often invisible to the one called. The problem drinker, for instance, may know in his heart that alcohol is keeping him from fulfilling his vocation as a husband, a father, a worker, a channel of God's grace to his fellow man; he may even be on the brink of a fatal disease such as cirrhosis of the liver as a result of his drinking. And yet—such is the nature of the human mind and the nature of addiction—he is unable to see the real change that needs to be made. He pretends to himself and even before God that drinking is unrelated to his problems. Like the cross of the self-blind alcoholic, our crosses are right before our eyes if we will just see them: the obligation to overcome anger, the requirement to pray for our enemies, the command to forgive others when hating them is so much more appealing, the obligation to stop criticizing and to build up the people in our lives instead of tearing them down. Even the need to be conscientious at work or frugal with our money can involve crosses of self-denial. Many divorces reflect a rejection of the cross.

Upon reflection, it is easy to see that members of Christ's Catholic Church are obligated to lift a special kind of cross—that of renouncing pagan solutions to moral questions. Far too many Catholics (one would be too many) have allowed themselves to be influenced in serious moral decisions by the spirit of our increasingly secular and pagan age rather than by the teaching of the Church. They have accepted the myths, for instance, that the world is "overpopulated" and that they as individuals have the absolute right to be self-determining. With these false ideas has come approval of contraception, fornication, divorce, and abortion. Many young couples in the Catholic Church live together before being married. Their poor marriage preparation leads to their becoming divorce statistics, for 70 percent of "trial marriages" fail.[12] Divorce and fornication have been greatly encouraged by the acceptance of contraception, just as Pope Pius XI foresaw seventy

---

[12] Michael McManus, "Veil of Tears," *Policy Review*, Winter 1994.

years ago.[13] And many of the crimes committed by fatherless young men in our urban ghettoes—especially drug dealing and murder—can be traced back to these factors as well.

It may seem strange to call avoidance of these sins a "cross," but that is just what it is. We must crucify the urge to accept sinful worldly solutions to problems of faith and morals. We may not allow ourselves the false luxury of thinking and doing just as everyone else does. We are required to take up this cross by renouncing that privilege, even if we find it inconvenient, embarrassing, or threatening to our selfish way of life. We are required to look to the divinely guided teaching authority of the Church to which we belong for moral and doctrinal guidance. Only then can we be the salt of the earth and the light of the world instead of being part of the surrounding rot and darkness. Only then will we be imitating the Lord, who bore our transgressions on his back.

Mary on the Via Dolorosa. Our Lady has heard of the verdict and the sentence of death. She follows Christ as he goes to his execution. She takes the back streets, a short cut to the path that she knows he will traverse. She knows that nothing practical can be gained by her seeing him, yet she places herself where the meeting is inevitable. Her eyes meet his and, helpless and desperate with grief, she takes her own way to Golgotha.

Suggested intentions. Jesus calls on us to pick up our personal crosses and follow him. Each of us has manifold crosses to carry. That which he asks us to bear at a given moment may be merely a small act of self-denial. It may, on the other hand, involve great suffering. Whatever it is, we should pray that we will recognize God's will for us at all times and ungrudgingly carry it out. Thus will we lift our crosses and follow in his footsteps.

---

[13] Pius XI, *Casti Connubii*, 1930.

5

THE CRUCIFIXION

Littera: Scripture and gloss. The Gospel accounts of the Crucifixion are appallingly brief, especially if one takes *crucifixion* in the
narrow sense: the actual nailing and raising up of the victim. According to St. Luke, when the soldiers came with Jesus to Golgotha,
"they crucified him there as well as the criminals, one on his right
and one on his left" (Luke 23:33). St. John writes, "There [on
Golgotha] they crucified him, and with him two others, one on
either side, while Jesus was in the middle" (John 19:18). St. Mark
mentions the offer of a weak anaesthetic: "They tried to give him
wine mixed with myrrh; but he did not take it" (Mark 15:23). St.
Matthew adds another element, to which the Revised Standard
Version (following the Greek and the Vulgate) grammatically sub-
ordinates the Crucifixion itself: "They offered him wine to drink,
mingled with gall; but when he tasted it, he would not drink it.
And when they had crucified him, they divided his garments among
them by casting lots; they sat down and kept watch over him there"
(Matthew 27:34-36).

Further context. The context of the actual deed of crucify-
ing Jesus includes what happened afterward, while he was suspended between heaven and earth. His utterances during that time
are known as the "Seven Last Words of Christ." In addition to
them, several events are recorded in Scripture.

One might think that in the Lord's chosen situation he could
do nothing besides remain stationary and wait to die. But the first

of his utterances from the cross, far from being mere words, bespoke an *action*, though a mental and spiritual one, of universal consequence. He implored God about his executioners and those who had brought him to Calvary, "Father, forgive them, for they do not know what they are doing" (Luke 23:34). This prayer, recorded by St. Luke as coming immediately after Jesus was lifted up, reveals his frame of mind—a completely selfless desire for the spiritual welfare of his tormentors—and points to the great miracle of forgiveness being accomplished. We have seen Jesus in a state of "righteous anger" before, when he drove the moneychangers from the Temple (Matthew 21:12-13, Mark 11:15, John 2:14-17).[14] But at that time he was reacting to the merchants' disrespect for the Temple, the house of his Father. The situation at the Crucifixion is quite different. At the Crucifixion, where Jesus himself is the target of violence, he offers no resistance and does not resort to anger of any kind. Humanly speaking we would expect anger, bitterness, retaliatory words. Instead, as the prophet Isaiah wrote of the Suffering Servant, "like a sheep that before its shearers is dumb, so he opened not his mouth" (Isaiah 53:7)—at least not in anger or recrimination or self-pity. Instead, he opened it in forgiveness. And because his entire Passion was undertaken for the forgiveness of man's sins, this first utterance on the cross is profoundly appropriate. It means that, as the last chapter of his earthly life begins, the Anointed One is perfectly fulfilling his earthly vocation. His saying is not mere words. It represents an astonishingly bounteous

---

[14] The ascription of emotions to God has always been troublesome. St. Augustine makes it clear that when men speak of the wrath of God, they are speaking figuratively (see, for instance, *De doctrina christiana*, trans. D.W. Robertson [New York: Bobbs Merrill, 1958], p. 89)—using terminology that applies only figuratively to God in order to make a point. God is not passible and therefore cannot have emotions. This fact is very significant in the definition of love, for it means that since God is love, love is not an emotion but something else—an act of the will. When Jesus is angry in the Temple, however, he is proving that he is perfectly human as well as perfectly divine. As a human being, he can be affected by emotion, though he remains without sin.

act of forgiveness on the part of God himself—the great grace that at long last, now, at the death of the Savior, remitted Adam's sin and reversed the Fall of man. Consequently, like other sayings on the cross, the prayer for forgiveness has meaning for all mankind, not just for those present. We can all be sure that, just as we took part through our sins in the Crucifixion of Jesus,[15] we are also beneficiaries of his boundless forgiveness.

We likewise share in a profound sense in the second of his "words," addressed to Mary and John in the Gospel of St. John. Again the scene is greatly abbreviated. It is as if the only details about Jesus' time on the cross recorded in this Gospel are those that John himself witnessed. Nevertheless, some of them are among the most important details in Scripture. St. John writes,

> Now standing by Jesus' cross were his Mother, and his Mother's sister, Mary the wife of Clopas, and Mary Magdalene. When Jesus saw his Mother and the disciple whom he loved standing by, he said to his Mother, "Woman, here is your son!" Then he said to the disciple, "Here is your mother!" And from that hour the disciple took her into his own home (John 19:25-27).

In this passage all Christians are invited to stand in St. John's shoes, as Jesus, in decreeing a marvelous spiritual adoption, declares the Blessed Virgin's motherhood of Christians—and indeed of all men. The Blessed Virgin's "maternal role was extended and became universal on Calvary."[16] As I have discussed in connection with the Annunciation, the "spiritual maternity" of Mary really dates from her obedient response to the angel Gabriel's announcement:

---

[15] When on Good Friday we sing the spiritual "Were you there when they crucified my Lord?" we can change the syntax and pronouns to reflect the truth: "I was there when we crucified our Lord."

[16] Pope Paul VI, *Marialis Cultus*, February 2, 1974, no. 37.

when Jesus became man at the moment of his conception, all human beings became his siblings and his Mother became theirs. The Incarnation is itself a kind of adoption, in which the Lord Jesus represents all human beings. It follows that his Mother is Mother of us all. But the scene at the cross goes further, for it explicitly ratifies this spiritual adoption. Just as important, it implicitly invites all Christians to venerate the Blessed Virgin. There is great love in this scene: the love of the Firstborn for his desolate Mother, his love for John, but also the Lord's love for all of us, to whom he commends the holy Virgin as our own Mother. It is our Catholic faith that Mary forthwith spiritually adopted every one of us. Whereas the brotherhood of man is included in the Incarnation, the brotherhood of disciples is included in this scene at Calvary, where St. John is a sort of metonym for the Church. Because we all become Mary's sons and daughters in the person of St. John—closer to her than non-Christians, just as the Church is closer to her—we invite her into our homes and become obedient to her; while, for her part, the Blessed Virgin takes on the role of our loving Mother and perpetual helper. Would that all people might be so close to her as loyal Catholics are.

In some respects the "adoption" scene at the cross is contrapuntal to the wedding at Cana, where Jesus turned water into wine (John 2:1-11). At that first miracle, as in the latter scene, he calls his Mother "woman," an address that lends universality to her significance—as if she symbolically represented all women. At Cana he tells her, "My hour has not yet come," thus expressing a reluctance to begin his public ministry, or at least the ministry of "signs," which is so important to St. John. The Blessed Mother shows by her advice that she is aware of his powers: "Do whatever he tells you," she bids the servants. These words should stand for her testament to us on behalf of Jesus: "Do whatever he tells you." At the Crucifixion scene, by contrast with Cana, the Lord's "hour" has certainly come. The time for his miracles is over, however, or at least temporarily suspended. The "signs" that Jesus has wrought have sufficed to convince his followers of his divine origin, even if they have notably failed to convince his detractors. Now, on the brow of Golgotha, he must go through the non-miraculous, universal, human act of dying. It pleased the divine wisdom to receive this precious sacrifice, not to forestall it by miraculous intervention. Jesus must die at Calvary. There, Mary is quiet, stunned to silence by the torture and death of her Son.

Christ's next utterance on the cross is directed to the "good thief":

> One of the criminals who was hanging blasphemed him and said, "Are you not the Messiah? Save yourself and us!" But in response the other rebuked him and said, "Do you not fear God?—you are under the same sentence! And we justly; for we are being paid back fittingly for what we did; but this man has done nothing wrong." And he said, "Jesus, remember me when you come into your kingdom." Jesus said to him, "Amen, I say to you, this day you will be with me in Paradise" (Luke 23:39-43).

The two criminals epitomize the attitudes of the witnesses on Calvary. One group, the larger, is a violent mob of uncomprehending Jews and Roman soldiers who ridicule the Lord as he hangs dying. So does the "bad thief." The other group, quieter and smaller, comprises the few stunned disciples of Christ who dared to come out, including his Mother. We don't know how strong the faith of this group was at this dark hour. Did most of the followers of the Lord retain some faith in his promises in spite of what they saw, or did they sadly give up hope? Did any of them really understand his promise to rise from the dead? In any case, just as the phrase "good thief" is apparently self-contradictory, the criminal who defended Jesus turns out to be on the side of the angels. His words to the Lord are an expression of faith in the success of Jesus' mission. The disciples, including St. Peter, don't seem to comprehend the Res-urrection. Nor, for that matter, do the criminal's words indicate any clear idea of that glorious event. Nevertheless, his prayer to Jesus bespeaks *some* kind of faith in the Lord's supernatural power. We don't know what the criminal is thinking. Probably he doesn't either. But we do know that he expresses confidence in the words of this "King of the Jews" hanging beside him. For that reason—and because he recognizes the moral realities of his own situation and those of Jesus and the other thief—the Lord promises him a place in Paradise "this day." Past actions, no matter how evil, are forgiven in the Lord's magnanimity. God's love overcomes all sin.

We come now to a group of sayings that cluster toward the end of Christ's time on the cross. One of these, reported in Mark and Matthew, and another reported in Luke, were uttered at about the "ninth hour," that is, 3:00 P.M., the time of the Lord's death. The other two, reported in John, also occur just before Jesus dies, although John doesn't mention the time. All three of the Synoptic Gospels (Matthew, Mark, and Luke) mention that the sky was darkened from the sixth hour to the ninth. Thus did the Crucifixion, the supreme product of darkened minds, infect nature; thus did creation mourn the human death of the Creator.

To the end, the humanity of the Lord is painfully displayed in the Gospels. This fact makes those heresies that deny the real-ity of Christ's human nature seem very strange. In particular, in addition to his subjection to suffering and death in general, St. John tells us a moving detail about the misery of the cross:

> After this, Jesus, knowing that everything had already been accomplished, in order to fulfill the scripture, said, "I'm thirsty." There was a container there full of sour wine; so after putting a sponge full of the sour wine on some hyssop they held it up to his mouth (John 19:28-29).

The pain in his arms and legs and diaphragm (not to mention his lacerated back) is momentarily less than the discomfort of thirst, and the Lord gives voice to this suffering: "I'm thirsty." It is evidently not the words that fulfill the Scripture, however, but the fact of his thirst and of the sour wine or vinegar. Psalm 22:15 may be the passage referred to: "my strength is dried up like a potsherd, and my tongue cleaves to my jaws; thou dost lay me in the dust of death." Significantly, according to Matthew and Mark, Jesus quotes the beginning of this psalm when he is near death and feeling forsaken by his Father. Perhaps John does not quote it because he didn't hear it. Nevertheless, he has in mind *some* Old Testament passage, and this one seems quite appropriate.[17]

Hyssop is a plant with branches that are convenient for sprinkling liquids. In particular, it is used in the Old Testament for ritual cleansing, often by sprinkling the blood of sacrificial animals. In Psalm 51:6 it sounds as if the hyssop itself rather than the liquid is the cleansing agent ("Purge me with hyssop, and I shall be clean; wash me, and I shall be whiter than snow"), though the psalmist may have transferred the agency from the liquid to the sprinkler. Eusebius notes hyssop as a seasoning.[18] In the Roman world vinegar or sour wine came in a weak, potable type, which was actually used as a beverage, and in a strong, less potable type. Surely Jesus is offered the strong type; otherwise it would not be remarkable.

---

[17] I am aware that most Scripture scholars now consider belief in the reportorial nature of the Gospels to be naive. But I believe that even if, as they say, the Gospels reflect the word-of-mouth traditions of various communities of believers, some of whom followed St. John and some of whom followed the other evangelists, nevertheless the narrative is based on the actual witness of John and the others. Not all scholars accept the modern schema, of course, even for the Gospel of John. The variety of details presented in the different Gospels suggests a multiplicity of points of view on the part of *actual witnesses*, whose first-hand accounts of the life of Christ are, the Church teaches, absolutely reliable (see, for instance, Vatican II, *Dei Verbum*, no. 11). When you get down to it, it takes a good deal of naivete to think that "communities" as such write books.

[18] Eusebius, op. cit., 155.

Both Matthew and Mark relate what is perhaps the most poignant of Jesus' utterances on the cross. The two accounts are about equally circumstantial. St. Mark writes:

> At the ninth hour Jesus cried with a loud voice, "*Eloi, Eloi, lama sabach-thani?*" which means, "My God, my God, why have You forsaken me?" Some of the bystanders heard it and said, "See, he's calling Elijah!" And someone ran and, filling a sponge full of sour wine, put it on a reed and gave it to him to drink, saying, "Let's see if Elijah is coming to take him down" (Mark 15:33-36).

The Incarnation and passibility of Jesus go no further than this: that the Son of God not only became subject to pain and death, but that while he was suffering, his human misery evidently overcame his hope and sense of mission, at least for the moment, so that he thought himself forsaken. Nailed up on the cross, Jesus received no comfort from a human touch or loving voice. Facing death alone regardless of the crowd, he felt deserted by the Father and cried out in his desolation. His words, quoted from the beginning of Psalm 22, again emphasize his connection with the suffering figures of the Old Testament. They amount to an interpretation of such passages as Psalm 22 as messianic prophecies. Such interpretations give us the true, veiled meaning of much of the Old Testament. Who would know better than Jesus the meaning of the Scriptures? Who can better lift the veil?

With the greatest humility Jesus undergoes this lonely human death. And with equally great arrogance and stupidity—such arrogance and stupidity as you and I might have shown if we had been there—his auditors misunderstand his words and treat him as a sort of laboratory specimen: "Let's watch to see if Elijah is coming to take him down." Much that they have done is a fulfillment of prophecy—throwing dice for his garments, piercing his hands and feet, giving him vinegar to drink. Unwittingly, in all these activities they urge the divine mission toward its accomplishment. St. Luke, however, records a more hopeful saying:

> It was already about the sixth hour, and darkness came over the whole land until the ninth hour, the sun's light having failed, while the sanctuary curtain was torn down the middle. And Jesus called out with a loud voice and said, "Father, into Your hands I entrust my spirit!" And after saying this he died (Luke 23:44-46).

This is obviously the final utterance that Luke attributes to the Lord before his death. St. John heard a later one. The Lucan saying stands in sharp contrast to the cry of "forsaken." In it Jesus expresses the exhaustion of his human resources and his final recourse to the Father. When all ability to control one's life is perforce relinquished to circumstance, all men must admit their powerlessness. Any other attitude is based upon a delusion, a denial of one's mortality. When the Lord entrusts his spirit to the Father, he echoes the awareness of the psalmist: "Truly no man can ransom himself, or give to God the price of his life" (Psalm 49:7). That being the case, he resigns himself to the Father's will. Such surrender embodies the great spiritual paradox of life-through-death, the hope that Jesus extends to his followers: "Whoever would save his life will lose it, while whoever loses his life for my sake will find it" (Matthew 16:25). Jesus blazes this trail and bids us to follow him. On a daily and nightly basis we should commit the keeping of ourselves, soul and body, to the Father. Such a practice not only maintains in us a proper sense of our own absolute dependence, but also prepares us for the moment of death, when we should throw ourselves into the arms of God with complete trust and abandon. If invited, Mary will be there to help us do this.

The final saying on the cross is usually interpreted as the Lord's comment on his own mission. It is recorded by St. John as coming just after the expression of thirst and the vinegar-filled sponge: "When he took the sour wine, Jesus said, 'All has been fulfilled,' and bowed his head and gave up his spirit" (John 19:30). The Lord looked upon the difficult task that he had undertaken and, undoubtedly with great relief, proclaimed it "fulfilled," "finished," "consummated." He had long known that he was to give his life, as his earlier communication with his disciples indicates. The fear of the actual sacrifice, with its attendant pain, mockery, and human fear of death formed part of the agony in Gethsemane. And now, finally, at Calvary the great deed is accomplished.

Three final events must be mentioned in the context of the Crucifixion. According to all three Synoptic Gospels (Matthew 27:51, Mark 15:38, and Luke 23:45), when Jesus died, the veil or curtain of the Temple sanctuary was ripped from top to bottom— undoubtedly a miraculous occurrence meaning that the Holy of Holies had changed locales and was henceforth to be located in the person of Jesus himself and in the sacraments mediated by his Church. At that time it became evident that the Holy of Holies in the Temple was a foreshadowing image of the new Holy of Holies. After the death and Resurrection of Christ, the people of God enter the Holy of Holies by being joined with their new High Priest, who once and for all time entered the inner sanctum and remains there eternally to intercede for us (Hebrews 8 and 9). This is as the Lord said. Jesus himself had taught that the "hour is coming … when the true worshipers will worship the Father in spirit and truth" (John 4:23)—that is, not in any particular place such as the Temple, but through the sacrifice of "a broken and contrite heart" (Psalm 51:17) offered to the Father in union with the Son's sacrifice. The focal point of that offering is the Eucharist.

With the rending of the Temple veil came another event, also reported by the first three Gospels. When the centurion, or Roman commander of 100 soldiers—evidently the very one who had been in charge of the Crucifixion—witnessed the Lord's deportment on the cross and the events that surrounded his holy death, he said, "Truly this man *was* the Son of God!" (Matthew 27:54, Mark 15:39). Luke's version says, "This man really was innocent!" (Luke 23:47). The discrepancy can be explained by St. Matthew, who records that a plurality of observers exclaimed at the death of Jesus. The utterances therefore included that of the centurion and of other men (soldiers?) standing by. Different observations were expressed, and two different ones were recorded. Surely, if the whole scene had been recorded, a large number of concluding observations would have been written. The centurion's realization as given in Luke is, of course, an admission that the officer has just killed an innocent man. Pilate had already admitted as much, while cynically sentencing the Lord to death. The centurion, who merely carries out orders, is less blameworthy. The larger claim in Matthew and Mark reflects a more profound realization: that the victim was indeed the Son of God. If the good thief's prayer indicates a similar realization, then the soldier and the criminal are here joined together in a classless bond of faith, however undeveloped. St. Paul's later teaching that in Christ "there is neither Jew nor Greek, there is neither slave nor free, there is neither male nor female," but all are "one in Christ Jesus" (Galatians 3:28) is unintentionally foreshadowed here. The thief entered Paradise that day. The centurion confessed the divinity of Christ, and who knows where this recognition led?

A third event is recorded only by Matthew (27:51-53). After the Temple veil was torn,

> the earth was shaken, and the rocks were torn apart and the tombs were opened, and many bodies of the saints who had fallen asleep arose, and they came out of the tombs after his resurrection and went into the holy city and appeared to many people.

These remarkable occurrences both foreshadow the Resurrection of Jesus and take place after it. Matthew's account of the earthquake and its aftermath indicates that in his own death and resurrection, "Jesus Christ the faithful witness, the firstborn of the dead and the ruler of kings on earth" (Revelation 1:5) seems to render the wall between life and death permeable so that it is traversed both ways by a number of people who had led holy lives. This scene also suggests and perhaps helped to inspire the story of the Harrowing of Hell, which will be discussed in the next chapter.

Extensions and applications. Writing about the Crucifixion is difficult because words pale in face of the reality. Just as the saints—Thomas Aquinas, for instance—have testified, to be on one's knees before the cross is better than any amount of clever observation or talk of any sort. What does one say before the overwhelming fact of Christ's sacrifice? Can any words adequately describe the Virgin's sorrow? Or can any discourse sum up the significance of the Passion? Can any superlatives accurately characterize the cross, the true axis of world history?

A few historical details about the nature of crucifixion are available. We are told by scholars that ropes were customarily used as well as nails to keep the victim up, for the nails alone would not suffice to hold up the body. Despite all of the depictions of Christ on the cross, the Romans evidently stripped the condemned man naked before putting him up. So much the greater humiliation; being naked before a crowd is the stuff of nightmares. We are also told that the cross did not extend far above the earth, that the sponge with sour wine or vinegar could have been lifted to the sufferer's mouth on a short stick. In some of the most beautiful portrayals of the event, the cross towers above the surrounding countryside. Though this depiction may not be historically accurate, in its figurative meaning the cross is very high, for it represents the consummation of Jesus' self-giving. After it he had nothing more to give, humanly speaking. The cross is the altar that pierces the heavens to lift the ultimate sacrifice to the Father. The artistic tradition in portrayals of the Crucifixion is based on this reality—the meaning of the cross in *salvation* history—not on a realistic depiction of Roman execution customs. On the cross human nature is lifted up to the Creator and restored to heavenly favor.

Because of that, tall or short, the cross is the most prominent symbol of Christendom. Christians used the sign of the cross at least as early as the late second century, and probably from the very earliest days of the Church, to identify themselves as Christians and as an adjunct to prayer. The three points of the top and arms early lent themselves to signifying the Holy Trinity. In the earliest Church the sign of the cross was traced on candidates for baptism and confirmation, as now. The cross came to adorn churches, altars, statuary, grave markers, coats of arms, banners, weapons, furniture, books, necks, ears, bishops' signatures, cars, and just about everything associated with the lives of Christians. In our era, unfortunately, the cross has even come to be a chic article of apparel that doesn't necessarily signify anything about its wearer. A great pity.

The saving action of Jesus on the cross is the only hope for the world, for his sacrifice is a type of the self-renunciation that is necessary for salvation, not as an "ideal" but as a simple fact. Every human being who wants to find God must go through this self-effacement or the quest will be in vain. Such self-sacrifice entails an honest striving to know and do the will of God, and to correct one's own will by the divine will. Though the Church teaches very clearly that one does not have to be a formally enrolled Catholic in order to attain salvation,[19] she teaches just as clearly that all salvation comes through faith in Christ,[20] even if it is unrecognized faith. Because of *his* sacrifice, the sacrificial love and self-giving

---

[19] Vatican II, for instance, in *Unitatis redintegratio* (Decree on Ecumenism), teaches: "[A]ll who have been justified by faith in baptism are incorporated into Christ" (no. 2).

[20] *Catechism of the Catholic Church*, no. 161.

actions of all people who seek God—Buddhists, Muslims, Hindus, Animists, non-Catholic Christians, and anyone else who desires to know and do God's will—will bring salvation. Jesus on the cross is still the channel through which all men are reconciled with the Father, whether consciously or unconsciously, for just as words of forgiveness flowed from his lips while he hung there, the stream of blood and water flowed from his side for the salvation of all who seek God. May we always remain in that saving stream.

Mary at the Crucifixion. The death of Jesus is the culminating pain for Our Lady of Sorrows. It is also a "decisive moment in the history of salvation."[21] Not only does the Crucifixion perfect Christ's sacrifice, it also provides the scene for his gift to the Church and the human race of his holy Mother, both as intercessor and as model. At Calvary, Mary becomes "an intercessor mighty in favor with God ... merciful enough to lift up again towards hope in the divine mercy the afflicted and the broken down."[22] Included in the gift of Mary as Mother is the tacit indication that she is "the model to be followed."[23]

Suggested intentions. All the pain in the world is comprehended in the suffering of Jesus. In his wounds we are all saved—if we do not reject his grace by our thoughts, words, and deeds. Let us pray that we and all for whom we pray will receive the benefit of this greatest of sacrifices and be brought to eternal life through the wounds of Christ. Let us ask Our Lady of Sorrows to help us focus our attention daily on the cross.

---

[21] Pope Paul VI, *Marialis Cultus*, no. 7.

[22] Pope Leo XIII, *Octobri Mense* (On the Rosary), September 22, 1891, no. 4.

[23] Pope Paul VI, *Signum Magnum*, May 13, 1967.

Chapter Four

THE GLORIOUS MYSTERIES

*T*he Glorious Mysteries "are the means
by which in the soul of a Christian a most clear light is
shed upon the good things, hidden to sense,
but visible to faith, 'which God has prepared
for those who love Him.'"

Pope Leo XIII

The first three Glorious Mysteries form an extended lesson on the triumph of Christ. The last two teach what that triumph means to the faithful human soul, of which the prime exemplar is Mary. From his victorious Resurrection, which forever proved his power to save, to his ascension into heaven, by which he took his place as the "only mediator between God and man," to his sending of the Holy Spirit, who guarantees that Christ will permanently guide the Church, the first three Glorious Mysteries attest to the Son's glorification after his obedience in the hour of darkness. Because he is man, his rising bodily from the dead portends the general destiny of the human race: we are all going to rise from the dead, some to an eternity of misery and some to an eternity of joy in God's presence. In the last two mysteries, the Blessed Virgin illustrates how eternal glory comes to the individual who strives to learn and to obey the will of God, no matter what the apparent cost. For her faithfulness to this vocation, and having no sin for which to atone, Mary was assumed into heaven and crowned Queen. She calls us to follow her in doing whatever Christ tells us.

The Glorious Mysteries bid us judge ourselves and our relation to the world by the light of eternity. They remind us of what we can be if we accept God's grace and, like the Blessed Virgin, live in his presence. More than a hundred years ago, the Holy Father taught that meditation on the Glorious Mysteries will protect the children of Mary from ever giving themselves completely to earthly goods. "We may doubt," wrote Leo XIII, "if God could inflict upon man a more terrible punishment than to allow him to waste his whole life in the pursuit of earthly pleasures, and in forgetfulness of the happiness which alone lasts forever. It is from this danger that they will be happily rescued who ... keep before their minds the Glorious Mysteries."[1]

On glory. But what is glory, and what does it mean for a mystery to be glorious? It is easy to see how joy is an attribute of the Joyous Mysteries and how it is attributed to the Blessed Virgin in them. It is also clear why the Sorrowful Mysteries convey sadness and why their sorrow belongs to the Virgin. But glory is another matter, much less obvious in its meaning. A look at some scriptural uses of the word *glory* will shed light on how the adjective *glorious* applies to the five Glorious Mysteries of the Rosary.

First, the term often applies to sought-after earthly things. Glory is associated with wealth in Psalm 49:16: "Be not afraid when one becomes rich, when the glory of his house increases." It is applied to the brilliant array and power of armies: "the Lord is bringing up against them the waters of the river, mighty and many, the king of Assyria and all his glory" (Isaiah 8:7). Earthly splendor in general is said to be glory, as in the Lord's comparison of Solomon's finery with a lily: "even Solomon in all his glory was not arrayed like one of these" (Matthew 6:29).

This association with beauty leads naturally to the constant linking of glory with light, as in the angelic announcement to the shepherds of the birth of Christ: "an angel of the Lord appeared to them, and the glory of the Lord shone around them, and they were greatly afraid" (Luke 2:9). In one of his visions the prophet Ezekiel saw how "the glory of the Lord went forth from the threshold of the house, and stood over the cherubim" (Ezekiel 10:19). When someone is said to have "a glory" about his head, a halo is meant. The use of light in most paintings of the Adoration of the Magi or

---

[1] Pope Leo XIII, *Laetitiae Sanctae*, September 8, 1893, nos. 8 and 9.

the Rest on the Flight to Egypt illustrates this meaning eloquently; the baby Jesus illumines the faces of those who surround him.

Several additional meanings of *glory* center around the ideas of merit, reputation, and praise. The Lord promises a loss of renown to his disobedient people: "I will change their glory into shame" (Hosea 4:7). In Scripture, praise is often made equivalent to glory: "From the ends of the earth we hear songs of praise, of glory to the Righteous One" (Isaiah 24:16). This meaning, though more limited, is closely related to the idea of the *glory of God*, to which I will return shortly. Very importantly, that which is meritorious is often made equal to glory. Sometimes *pride* (i.e., that of which one is proud) is a synonym, though not usually in a derogatory sense. Proverbs 20:29, for instance, states, "The glory of young men is their strength, but the beauty of old men is their grey hair." When the Israelites forsook the true God, they abandoned their meritorious state for a shameful one: "my people have changed their glory for that which does not profit" (Jeremiah 2:11). It should be noted, however, that anytime one's pride or sense of accomplishment prevents the proper praise of God, the pride is sinful, the glory quickly becomes vainglory.

All of the legitimate senses of *glory* are often and easily transferred to God and his attributes, to which I now turn. Glory is the natural right of the Creator. The magnificent Psalm 95 states the natural obligation of a creature to his Creator: "Come, let us worship and bow down, let us kneel before the Lord, our Maker!" God is the source of all lesser forms of glory—of light, of honor, of power, of all that is good, including being itself. As the all-powerful, all-knowing, and all-beneficent maker of the universe, God receives by right all the efforts of man. Therefore, very often in Scripture the phrase *glory of God*, or some equivalent, designates the whole proper end of human thought and effort. St. Paul exhorts the Corinthians, "Whether you eat or drink or whatever you do, do everything for the glory of God" (1 Corinthians 10:31).

Since nothing outside of God himself can do justice to his majesty and goodness, the mere human language of praise is always inadequate. Nevertheless, Scripture abounds with inspired admonitions to glorify God and examples of how to do so. The beauty and order of creation bespeak the worthiness of the Creator: "The heavens are telling the glory of God, and the firmament proclaims his handiwork" (Psalm 19:1). The miracles of Christ are performed for the same purpose. When Lazarus is mortally ill, for instance, Jesus points to the lesson to come: "This sickness will not bring death—it is for the glory of God, so that the Son of God may be glorified through it" (John 11:4). (An alternate lesson, that Jesus was making himself equal to the Father by performing "signs" that showed him to be God's Son, would not have been lost to his hearers.) The whole life of Christ glorified the Father, and the Glorious Mysteries tell how the Father in turn glorified the Son.

1

THE RESURRECTION

Littera: Scripture and gloss. Jesus is laid in a rock tomb belonging to a man named Joseph, from the Jewish village of Arimathea. Mark and Luke testify that Joseph was "looking forward to the kingdom of God" (Mark 15:43, Luke 23:51). This language verbally allies Joseph with the seers at the Presentation, Simeon and Anna, who see in Jesus the fulfillment of the covenant. Matthew and John go further and state that Joseph was a follower of Christ (Matthew 27:57, John 19:38). John adds that Joseph kept his discipleship quiet "for fear of the Jews." All four Gospels record that Joseph asked for the body of Jesus. This request suggests that, like Simeon and Anna, he saw the coming of the kingdom in the person of Jesus; hence his discipleship. Joseph wants to give the Lord an honorable burial. After his death, Jesus is taken from the cross, anointed, wrapped in a shroud, placed in Joseph's tomb, and sealed and guarded. Thus ended the events of that first Good Friday, which set the stage for the greatest miracle since creation.

The gloom of Jesus' apparent failure and death must have seemed heavy to his disciples. Many must have despaired and dismissed the Lord and his teaching as just another blind alley. Even those who retained hope in him must have felt confounded in doubt. Granted that the late Prophet told the truth, they may have asked, *how* was his teaching true and what is to come of it? But then the Resurrection blew away the clouds of doubt and ignorance.

The Gospels relate the story of the Resurrection in four different but complementary accounts. St. Mark's is:

> And when the Sabbath was over, Mary Magdalene, and Mary the mother of James, and Salome, bought spices so that they could go and anoint him. And very early in the morning of the first day of the week they came to the tomb when the sun had risen. They were saying to each other, "Who will roll the stone away from the door of the tomb for us?" but when they looked up, they saw that the stone had been rolled away, for it was very large. When they went into the tomb, they saw a young man seated on the right hand side, dressed in a white robe; and they were astonished. But he said to them, "Do not be alarmed; you are looking for Jesus of Nazareth, who was crucified. He has risen; he is not here; look at the place where they laid him! But go, tell his disciples and Peter, 'He is going ahead of you into Galilee; you will see him there just as he told you." Then the women went out and fled the tomb; for trembling and amazement had seized them, and they said nothing to anyone, because they were afraid (Mark 16:1-8).

As one would expect, the Gospel accounts vary considerably in detail, depending on the point of view of the narrator. St. John, for instance, speaks as one who took part in the events, calling himself "the other disciple" who accompanied St. Peter to the tomb (John 20:4). Just as John has particularized his point of view toward Christ's pierced side and insisted on the truth of what happened (he himself saw the blood and water flow from the wound), here he offers convincing details about the unfolding drama: breathlessly impelled onwards, he outran the older Peter and looked into the tomb, but in deference to the leader of the apostles he allowed Peter to enter first. The emphasis on the position of the grave cloths is particularly circumstantial: "he [Peter] saw the linen cloths lying there, and the face covering, which had been on his head, not lying with the linen cloths but wrapped up separately in its own place" (John 20:6-7). After John entered, "he saw and believed." That belief was the beginning of the disciples' realization that Jesus had risen from the dead, for until the event itself and Christ's post-Resurrection appearances the idea of the Resurrection was not at all clear to them. They had heard him talk about it, but didn't know what he meant. Even when they found the empty tomb, they were just beginning to learn.

Some elements of the Resurrection accounts are common: the discovery of the empty tomb by the women who followed the Lord, the apostles' dawning realization of what Jesus had meant by talking about his Resurrection, the dramatic subsequent appearances of the Risen One. These provide much material for contemplation. By itself, the empty tomb could have meant that someone had stolen the body. But Christ showed himself alive to numerous witnesses—to Mary Magdalene (Mark 16:9), to the apostles (Matthew 28:16-17), to St. Thomas (John 20:24-29), to the disciples on the road to Emmaus (Luke 24:13-35), and to others.

What is the value of these witnesses' testimony? Do the Gospel writers and those of whom they speak seem credible? Yes! All of Christendom is raised on their sober testimony. The Gospel writers never sound crazy, and their accounts never look calculated to promote a lie. They don't describe the moment of the Resurrection itself—the restoration to life of the body of the Lord, instantaneously renewed and spiritualized. But this fact itself lends credibility to their account. It is very likely that a writer trying to promulgate a lie would have included some kind of account of this astonishing event. Likewise, the Gospel writers use no superlatives in claiming the reality of the Resurrection. Their tone is, rather, that of calm reportage. True, they report the excitement of St. Peter and St. John, of Mary Magdalene, and later of the other disciples; but they do so with no bluster. In no case, where witnessing to the Resurrection is the point, do the scriptural writers do what one would naturally expect of a lie monger.

As suggested, the Resurrection of Jesus is different from other biblical "resurrections." It is not a mere resuscitation of a dead body such as that which Lazarus had undergone. When Lazarus was raised, he was brought back to a former, still mortal, state. However miraculous his resuscitation may have been, Lazarus later died. He will rise again someday, and that will be his first and only true resurrection. Jesus, however, unlike Lazarus, truly rose from the dead; his mortal body was changed to a spiritual one, recognizably the same and yet different. We don't have even a faint idea what this transformation is like. We must simply take it on faith. And we know that it will also happen to us.

Further context. A prelude to the Resurrection is denoted by a phrase in the Apostles' Creed, "He descended into hell." The episode indicated, known popularly as the Harrowing of Hell, was for centuries included in the Christian story and in devotions. It expresses an essential aspect of the Passion of Christ and the redemption he brought to all men—the fact that the sacrifice of Jesus saves all who seek to know and serve God, both before and after the earthly life of Christ. The story of the Harrowing was perpetuated, for instance, in an apocryphal book known as the *Gospel of Nicodemus*, or *Acts of Pilate*.[2] In that book, after his death Jesus enters the realm of Satan to deliver Adam and the patriarchs from the grasp of the devil. At the thunderous words of Psalm 24, "Lift up your heads, O gates! and be lifted up, O ancient doors! that the King of glory may come in," the gates of hell are ripped open, the blinding light of Christ streams into the blackness of hell and smites the fearful devils' eyes, and the captive saints of old behold with adoration the King whose coming they had foretold. The Harrowing of Hell was also the subject of plays and poems in the Middle

---

[2] Montague Rhodes James, *The Apocryphal New Testament* (Oxford University Press, 1924; corrected 1953), pp. 94-165.

Ages. Though fanciful, the story contains a truth of faith that is worthy of mention, for after his Passion our Lord truly harrowed hell and conquered death.

The Resurrection transformation of Jesus is foreshadowed by his Transfiguration (Matthew 17:1-13, Mark 9:2-13, Luke 9:28-36). At that remarkable event, in the company of Peter, James, and John, the Lord changed appearance so that his clothes became intensely white, "as white as light," while two paramount ancient Jewish leaders, Elijah and Moses, appeared and spoke to him. The change in the Lord's appearance accords with other features of a theophany or manifestation of God in Scripture, notably the brightness of Moses' face after he talks to God (Exodus 34:29-35). So much can be said with assurance. But the full meaning of this symbolic scene is uncertain.

The change in the risen Christ's appearance, which makes him hard to recognize at first (cf. John 20:14, 21:4ff.), is also parallel to the change that all people will undergo at the general resurrection. Through St. Paul the Holy Spirit speaks of this transformation:

> Behold I will tell you a mystery—not all of us will die, but all of us will be transformed, in a moment, in the twinkling of an eye, at the sound of the last trumpet call. When the trumpet sounds, the dead will be raised imperishable and we shall be transformed. For this corruptible body must be clothed in incorruptibility, and this mortal body must be clothed in immortality. And when this corruptible body is clothed in incorruptibility ... then the following passage of Scripture will come to pass: "Death is swallowed up in victory" (1 Corinthians 15:51-54).

The "mortal body" and its attributes will be transformed, but not beyond recognition. After a moment Mary Magdalene and the apostles recognized Christ; his companions at Emmaus recognized him when he broke the bread (Luke 24).

It is certain that St. Peter and the other disciples took the Resurrection as the keystone of their faith. And small wonder, for all of the claimed divinity of Jesus rests upon it. The Virgin birth would have been just a mythical story, the miracles of Christ just tricks of a magician, his moral teaching just strange counter-cultural ideas, his theology the ravings of a lunatic (especially about himself as representative of the Creator and as the Bread of Life). These stones of the Christian faith remain firm because after his great trial and sacrifice, Jesus Christ demonstrated for all time that he *is* the Son of God, and in this demonstration he became the first of all mankind who will rise from the dead at the general resurrection. Except for his holy Mother, who was assumed into heaven without "seeing corruption" (cf. Psalm 16:10),[3] all human beings will rise on that day. We will see ourselves as we really are, in the unblinking light of Truth itself. Because of this, our judgment will coincide perfectly with the divine reality. God *will* judge us, but we will also judge ourselves—we will see and know that his judgment is both absolutely merciful and absolutely just, and we will ratify his judgment with this new-found knowledge. Those who rise in Christ will shine like the stars, and those who do not will recognize themselves as "an everlasting horror and disgrace," unfit for the divine presence (cf. Daniel 12:2).

In all the preaching of the early Church the Resurrection is the central theme. When it is not explicitly the topic, it is the fulcrum on which all the other matters turn. The exaltation of Christ in glory is repeatedly the subject of St. Peter's sermons to the very

---

[3] Psalm 16:10 is quoted and applied to Jesus in Acts 2:27 and 13:35, where Peter and Paul are preaching on the Resurrection of Christ. The Sacred Tradition of the Church also applies the idea to the Blessed Virgin Mary and codifies it in the doctrine of the Assumption.

people who had crucified the Lord. A representative example occurs in Acts 2:

> [Peter says] God raised this Jesus—of this we are all
> witnesses—and when he was exalted at the right hand of
> God and had received from the Father the promise of the
> Holy Spirit, he poured it forth, as you can see and hear.…
> Let the whole house of Israel know beyond any doubt—
> this Jesus whom you crucified, God made both Lord and
> Messiah (Acts 2:32-33, 36).

St. Paul begins his letter to the Roman Christians by pointing out
that Jesus Christ was "designated Son of God in power according
to the Spirit of holiness by his resurrection from the dead" (Romans 1:4). No other event could have accomplished this purpose
and so demonstrated the divinity of the one who came to bring
light to "those who sit in darkness and the shadow of death" (Luke
1:78).

The mysteries of the Resurrection, the Ascension, and the
Descent of the Holy Spirit are interlocked in the experience and
inspiration of the earliest Church. It is the raising of Jesus with
which St. Peter confronts the Jewish leaders and by which he converts many of them to Christ, for the Resurrection proves Jesus to
be the Messiah. It is the Ascension that enables the Lord, as he
himself says (John 16:7), to send the Holy Spirit upon the apostles.
And it is the gift of the Holy Spirit that transforms the disciples of
Christ from cowering midgets into courageous public witnesses to
their faith. Only by witnessing these three events and receiving
the divine influence intrinsic to them do the apostles come fully
to understand Christ's prophecies about his own Resurrection.

Extensions and applications. The Resurrection of Christ is
the turning point in the human struggle against death, a struggle
that man could never win without God's merciful intervention.

Whether personified or not, death has always been seen as an adversary by thoughtful people of all cultures, a lurking enemy who waits behind the scenes of one's life and ultimately wins. In the ancient Greek tragedy *Antigone*, for instance, Sophocles wrote:

> Wonders are many, and none is more wonderful than man: he has power to cross the white sea, driven by the stormy south-wind, plunging under surges that threaten to engulf him; and Earth ... does he master, turning the soil as the ploughs go to and fro year after year.... Yes, nothing is beyond his power; from baffling diseases he has devised escapes, and only against Death shall he call for help in vain.

Many of the most imposing monuments of ancient civilizations, as well as many relics of lesser-known peoples, reflect the human preoccupation with death: pyramids, funeral mounds, sarcophagi, provisions for the deceased, inscriptions, jewelry, innumerable elegiac literary works.

Seen in broad perspective, the death of Christ was an epic pitched battle between the Lord and the original curse of man. The advent of death on the human scene and its eventual abolition by Jesus Christ are, as some poets have seen, the ultimate epic material. The preeminent touchstones of human history—the fall of man into disorder, sorrow, and death and his redemption by Christ—are powerfully reflected, for instance, in the very titles of John Milton's *Paradise Lost* and *Paradise Regained*. The first man's sin—that aboriginal catastrophe—brought down upon the human race the darkness of death, and from that moment forth all human thought has been tinctured with the apprehension of mortality. Our first ancestors turned out the lights for all of us, and we have all since then been afraid of the dark. The Creator had warned Adam and Eve that if they ate of the "tree of the knowledge of good and evil" they would die (Genesis 2:17), and yet under the influence of Satan they freely and deliberately chose to consume the forbidden fruit. Whatever is symbolized by that powerful image, death thereby became certain—for them and for all the human race to come. Our first parents, whom God made of dust, were cursed to endure labor and pain and to return ultimately to the elements of which they were made (Genesis 3:19). What a diminution of "self-esteem" our first father must have undergone when he realized, however weakly, the enormity of his sin. Adam's curse has subsequently lain heavily upon all who have inherited his reduced spiritual stature, his new dimness of sight and perversion of will.

But death was never a part of God's good cosmos. It is a privation, a reduction of beings that were created good, not a positive creation in itself. It was caused by sin and not by God—by rebellious creatures who heeded not the rod of their Creator, and not by their Maker himself. "God did not make death," proclaims the book of Wisdom (1:13), and God never willed death upon mankind. But man was created free, and where there is freedom of will, consequences must be real; otherwise freedom is an illusion. Man has always been capable of reducing his own blessedness. This is a natural and inevitable consequence of God's great gift of freedom, a gift that God himself will not traduce. By his sin Adam deprived the human race of its original blessedness and thrust it into the night of sin and its bitter consequences. In that night the glimmer of heaven is dimmed, though it still brings pain to the feeble eye of the rebel. Jesus came to give rebels new eyes, to call them to the light that straightens the human will and overcomes the darkness. His Resurrection validates him as the dayspring from on high who gives "light to those who sit in darkness and in the shadow of death" (Luke 1:79). The mystery of the Resurrection thus fulfills the prophecy of the *Benedictus*.

Accepting Christ's Resurrection is tantamount to foreseeing our own. Jesus, fully human as he was, demonstrated a fact about human beings: that they are immortal. We, being human, are going to rise as he did. And, being sinful, we are going to be judged by him. Christ is called the "first fruits" of the general human resurrection, a term that metaphorically compares him with the first part of the harvest, which the Israelites always gave to God. The untold billions of other human beings are the rest of the harvest. St. Paul writes,

> As it is, Christ *was* raised from the dead, the first fruits of those who have died. For since death came through a man, resurrection from the dead *also* came through a man, for just as in Adam all die, so too in Christ they shall also come to life again. Each will be raised in the proper order: Christ the first fruits, then at his coming those who belong to Christ will rise. Then the end will come, when he will deliver the kingdom to his God and Father when he will do away with every ruler, authority and power. For Christ must reign until he has put all his enemies under his feet. The last enemy to be done away with will be death (1 Corinthians 15:20-26).

Jesus Christ will eventually destroy our death, as he vanquished his own. When that happens, we will be delivered from the travail brought on our race by Adam's sin.

We must not forget that Christ's Resurrection and exaltation at God's right hand came about after his *obedience* to the will of the Father. "Born in human likeness, and to all appearances a man, he humbled himself and became obedient, even unto death, death on a cross. For this reason God highly exalted him and gave him a name above every other name" (Philippians 2:8-9). What a difficult task Jesus accepted from the Father! How much pain and humiliation he underwent before, hanging on the cross, he could pronounce his mission finished! How averse his human nature was to the torture he endured! We all would like the resurrection without the cross. But, as the example of Jesus so clearly teaches, no struggle—no cross; no cross—no crown.

The empty tomb indicates also the bodily nature of Christ's Resurrection and therefore of the general resurrection. Some have the idea that the resurrection is merely a "spiritual" affair, not the resurrection of the body, and that the consciousness of the dead is forever disembodied. But if the promised resurrection is "spiritual" only, it isn't a resurrection at all, but a gathering of disembodied wraiths. If Jesus didn't rise from the dead bodily, then the empty tomb is no witness to his Resurrection. But such a belief is utterly at odds with Scripture and with the constant, firm, and clear teaching of the Church which holds that the soul is not a disembodied spirit but the "formative principle" of the body.[4] Bodiliness is part of the very definition of humanity; a human being is not a human being without a body, even if that body is a transformed, "spiritual" one. Presumably before the Fall man had a body like the resurrected one to come. Or, when the change from a mortal to an immortal body was to occur, the fear and loathing of death would have been absent. In any case each of us, according to the teaching of the Church, is to have a transformed body in eternity.

Granted, thoughtful people have had trouble conceiving *how* this is to be. Questions about just how one's body is to be reassembled for resurrection have abounded, and not just among children and opponents of Christianity. The most sophisticated early Christian writers gave quite a bit of thought to the matter. St. Paul addressed this matter in one of his letters to the Corinthians (1:35-50): "Perhaps someone will ask, 'How can the dead be raised? What kind of bodies will they have?'" Others have wondered, Can a body be radically changed in some spiritual way and still be the same body?[5] Such questions are worthwhile, for the pursuit of knowledge of all kinds is an exercise of man's godlike faculties. These

---

[4]   St. Thomas Aquinas, *Summa Theologiae*, 1a. 75,5.
[5]   See the fine study by Carolyn Walker Bynum, *The Resurrection of the Body* (New York: Columbia University Press, 1995).

questions were also inevitable as man came to understand his immortal nature and the nature of his world. In the final analysis, however, full and satisfactory answers to such questions remain far beyond all human capacity. We don't *really* understand even the simplest bodily processes. God's ways are not our ways, and his "foolishness" is above our wisdom.[6] Divine knowledge remains mysterious. What we as Christians do understand is that, according to abundant apostolic witness, the Lord has risen from the dead. Having thus proved himself God, he promised that we are also to rise. This is the promise of Christ's triumph over death and hell, which he shares with us.

Mary and the Resurrection. Mary learned about the Resurrection at second hand, but in a sense so did everyone else. Except perhaps for angels, the nearest possible other witness may well be a mysterious piece of cloth known as the Holy Shroud of Turin. Only through a relatively gradual process, in which Jesus presented himself alive to numerous witnesses, did his followers come to understand what had happened. In spite of her grief, Our Lady knew that somehow her Son would triumph. At his Resurrection that triumph became concrete.

Suggested intentions. (1) Because Jesus overcame death, death has been slain and will have no permanent dominion. All human beings, Jesus and Mary excepted, will arise on the last day to be judged for their thoughts, words, and deeds. Many other people depend, often without knowing it, upon our prayers. The Resurrection decade can therefore be fittingly offered for the souls of the dead to whom our own lives and prayers pertain—our fam-

---

[6] Cf. 1 Corinthians 1:25: "The foolishness of God is wiser than men, and the weakness of God is stronger than men." Also Isaiah 55:8: "My thoughts are not your thoughts, neither are your ways my ways, says the Lord."

ily members, people we have known, people whose deaths we learn about, our brothers and sisters in Purgatory. Let us pray for them: May the souls of the faithful departed by the mercy of God rest in peace. In addition, here or elsewhere, we should pray for dying sinners, remembering what Our Lady said at Fatima—that many souls are lost simply because no one prays for them. Those who are in mourning also need our prayers. (2) We should also pray that, as we are someday to rise physically from the dead, we may keep our bodies pure for God's judgment. The empty tomb of Christ bids us live chastely—against the day when we will all leave our tombs empty.

2

THE ASCENSION INTO HEAVEN

Littera and gloss. Only St. Mark and St. Luke record the actual Ascension of Christ into heaven. In St. Mark's version, Jesus addresses the eleven apostles who are left after Judas' defection and death. "The Lord Jesus, after speaking to them, was taken up into heaven, and took his seat at the right hand of God" (Mark 16:19). St Luke is more explicit about the setting: "Then he led them out to Bethany, and he lifted up his hand and blessed them. And it happened that as he was blessing them he parted from them, and was carried up to heaven" (Luke 24:50-51).

In both versions he is taken or carried up; he is lifted but does not lift himself. To the eyes of those present, he merely *ascends*. In St. Mark's version, his destination at the "right hand of God" the Father is specified. Thus Mark provides the origin of the affirmation in the Apostles' Creed that Jesus "sits at the right hand of God the Father almighty," and of the Nicene Creed that he "is seated at the right hand of the Father." What this means is that Jesus is the principal agent of the Divine in the world, for the right hand is figuratively the hand of strength and action.

Some, impatient with what they consider the naiveté of the Scriptures, have scorned the idea that Jesus actually *ascended*. Their complaint is based on their belief that heaven isn't "up" except in a figurative sense. Like many other sophists, they object to the presumed childishness of Scripture, whose authors seem to have thought of heaven as up and hell as down. But in so doing, such critics don't escape their own critique. They simply prove that they refuse to submit to the Gospel in a humble and childlike manner. The fact is that there is no way of describing the Lord's exit from the world without using figurative language. C.S. Lewis pointed this out long ago. This great Christian apologist wrote, "To say that God 'enters' the natural order involves just as much spatial imagery as to say that he 'comes down'; one has simply substituted horizontal (or undefined) for vertical movement. To say that he is 're-absorbed' into the Noumenal is better than to say he 'ascended' into heaven, only if the picture of something dissolving in warm fluid … is less misleading than the picture of a bird, or a balloon, going up. All language, except about objects of sense, is metaphorical through and through."[7] So Jesus may as well ascend as disappear in any other way, and the resulting account will still be the use of plodding human language to describe the indescribable—the transition (this is a metaphor, too) of the Lord from our three-dimensional world into a "world" (another metaphor) so different that human language can't capture it. Although the Lord wants us to use our brains, he also wants us to be receptive like little children, even if it means accepting scriptural narratives that some may consider naive. So learned a man as John Henry Newman is a good example here. The great cardinal accepted scriptural accounts of the supernatural with both an adult act of the will and the docility of a child. So should we all.

Further context. The short Gospel accounts of the Ascension appear in contexts rich with meanings, all of which are tied in with Christ's return to the Father. Jesus gives his disciples a solemn commission to carry out after he is gone. He then makes a great promise to his followers. Both the commission and the promise depend on the idea of his absence from his disciples and his

---

[7] C.S. Lewis, "Horrid Red Things," in *God in the Dock*, ed. Walter Hooper (Grand Rapids, Michigan: Eerdmans, 1970), p. 71.

presence with his Father. It would seem that the Ascension was necessary for the story of salvation to continue. The saving sojourn of Christ on earth was—and is—to be mysteriously completed by his Church.

The commission, often called the Great Commission, occurs in Mark and Matthew. St. Mark reports it thus: "And he said to them, 'Go into the whole world and proclaim the good news to all creation. Whoever believes and is baptized will be saved; but whoever does not believe will be condemned'" (Mark 16:15-16). St. Matthew combines the commission with the wonderful promise of Christ's continuing presence, as well as with specifications for administering the sacrament of Baptism:

> Jesus came to them and spoke to them and said, "All authority in heaven and on earth has been given to me. Go, therefore, and make disciples of all nations, baptizing them in the name of the Father and of the Son and of the Holy Spirit, and teach them to observe all that I have commanded you; and behold, I will be with you always until the end of the age" (Matthew 28:18-20).

"Until the end of the age" means, of course, "in perpetuity" or "until the end of the world." Christ's promised presence will never be withdrawn from his Church. In sacred history, the last age is the Christian era. God's revelation will never surpass or supplant the Incarnation of Christ, whose perpetually continued guidance of the Church will continue to enlighten human understanding until the end of the world. There will be no new ages in salvation history before the Second Coming.

The Great Commission is the marching orders for the Church, *all* of whose members are responsible for spreading the Gospel. The promise of divine help is made to the Church and to all her members who look to her for guidance. Though given foremost to the apostles and subsequent pastors (the bishops in union with the pope), the promise extends to all who strive to know and do God's will. It is fulfilled in the Church in the form of the special charism of infallibility, both in the ordinary Magisterium and in papal pronouncements that meet the criteria for infallibility (i.e., pronouncements made when the Holy Father teaches *ex cathedra* on decisions of faith and morals directed to the whole Church). The promise is fulfilled for Catholic individuals who call upon the name of the Lord and look with faith and obedience to the Church for guidance. This is precisely the character of the promise—that Jesus Christ will be with the *Church*, his Bride, who mediates his graces to her loyal children. Catholics who dissent from Church teaching are following some spirit besides the Spirit sent by Christ; they are in perilous waters, for all are called to religious adherence to the divinely guided Magisterium. Whoever listens to the bishops, the Second Vatican Council taught, "is listening to Christ and whoever despises them despises Christ and him who sent Christ."[8] All are called by the Great Commission to spread the Gospel in their own ways—to develop and use their talents, whether menial or intellectual or artistic, in such a way that the image of Christ will be seen in their lives. "The characteristic of the lay state being a life led in the midst of the world and of secular affairs, laymen are called by God to make of their apostolate, through the vigor of their Christian spirit, a leaven in the world."[9] Catholics who stay loyal to the teaching and practice of the Church may be sure that the Lord is with them in their effort. He has promised to do so.

The Ascension also set the stage for the transformation of the apostles from weak, half-believing men into courageous wit-

---

[8] *Lumen Gentium*, no. 20, in *Vatican II: The Conciliar and Post Conciliar Documents*, Study Edition, ed. Austin Flannery, O.P. (Northport, New York: Costello Publishing Company, 1987).

[9] *Apostolicam Actuositatem*, no. 2, in Flannery, op. cit.

nesses for Christ. Significantly, before the Great Commission in St. Mark's Gospel, Jesus "appeared to the eleven themselves as they reclined at table and reproached them for their unbelief and hardness of heart, because they had not believed those who had seen him after he had risen" (Mark 16:14). Faith came slowly. St. Thomas and others remained unconvinced until they *knew* of the Resurrection through visible and tactile proof. St. Thomas doesn't drop to his knees exclaiming "My Lord and my God!" until after he has received ocular proof of the Resurrection (John 20:24-29). But the fact that Jesus was definitively leaving, not to return again until the Second Coming, meant that such proof would never again be available. Consequently, the promise stated by St. Luke is overwhelmingly important for the Church.

At the end of Luke's Gospel, Jesus gave his apostles a final scriptural lesson. They had been so slow to learn. Now the Lord "opened their minds to understand the scriptures"—to know once and for all that he himself had been the chief hidden subject (and author) of the Old Testament, and that his life, death, and resurrection were to provide the substance of the preaching he commissioned them to do. Christ promised them the ability to be his witnesses in their teaching and sacrificial deaths (the word *martyr* comes from the Greek word for "witness"). The Lord promises this power in the context of his role as the subject of all of Scripture—what we now call the Old Testament. He tells the apostles,

> "Thus it is written, that the Messiah would suffer and rise from the dead on the third day, and that repentance and forgiveness of sins should be proclaimed in his name to all nations, starting from Jerusalem. You are witnesses of these things. And, behold, I am sending the promise of my Father upon you, so stay in the city until you are clothed with power from on high" (Luke 24:45-49).

Thus the Ascension sets the stage for Pentecost.

Extensions and applications. When Jesus ascended into heaven he entered the immediate presence of the Father, where he became the eternal intercessor, advocate, and high priest for all mankind. In his role as the new high priest he superseded the high priest of the Old Covenant, who had spoken principally for the Israelites. But Jesus has broken down the barriers of separation and now speaks for every member of the human race, for all are now called to be the people of God. The Lord could do this because of his Incarnation, by which he became the brother of every human being, just as Mary became our Mother by the same divine act and her own cooperation. The Church that Jesus founded is consequently the home of all people who hear his call, no matter their color or nationality.

By becoming human, God entered into human experience. He thus subjected himself to human emotion and to the reception of information, including pain, through human senses. In his Passion he underwent the suffering common to man and the concomitant temptations to which man is subject. Consequently, "we have not a high priest who is unable to sympathize with our weaknesses, but one who in every respect has been tempted as we are, yet without sinning" (Hebrews 3:15). By his Ascension, Jesus, who is *one of us*, stepped up to the judgment bar of God, where he pleads for us in our weakness. Pope Leo XIII underscores the meaning of the Ascension, which (with the other Glorious Mysteries) teaches "that the path to Heaven lies open to all men, and as we behold Christ ascending thither, we recall the sweet words of His promise, 'I go to prepare a place for you.'"[10] Though the Holy Spirit is usually called the Advocate, in his intercessory role Jesus is our representative in the court of heaven. In him we have the ultimate "friend in high places."

---

[10] *Laetitiae Sanctae*, no. 14.

The teaching of the Church on the Communion of Saints is partly derived from Christ's intercessory role. Just as Jesus intercedes for us, we can intercede for each other, always with the understanding that our prayer is channeled through Christ, the "one mediator between God and men" (1 Timothy 2:5). Jesus and the Holy Spirit, who "proceeds from the Father and the Son" (Nicene Creed), facilitate our prayers for each other. The Lord tells us to pray for our enemies and do good to them (Matthew 5:44). We are prone enough to pray for our loved ones, living and dead, without such a command. But the Lord wants us to do more—to act as intercessors even for our enemies. Moreover, the Church teaches that human intercessors are not limited to the living. Nor is intercession limited to the Lord, whose role as sole mediator is by no means diminished by the intercessory prayers of others. The lesser intercessors encompass all the saints who have gone before us, whose prayers for us bring gifts from the great "Treasury of Merit" stored up on our behalf and on behalf of those who, though lovers of God and right, do not know Christ. The intercession of Jesus is the prototype and the enveloping medium of all prayer to the Father. Mysteriously, that intercession became fully operative through the Ascension and the Lord's taking his seat at the "right hand of the Father."

Pope St. Leo the Great gives an inspiring theological interpretation of the Ascension:

> With all due solemnity we are commemorating that day on which our poor human nature was carried up, in Christ, above all the hosts of heaven, above all the ranks of angels, beyond the highest heavenly powers to the very throne of God the Father. It is upon this ordered structure of divine acts [i.e., the Resurrection followed by the Ascension] that we have been firmly established, so that the grace of God may show itself still more marvelous when, in spite of the withdrawal from men's sight of everything that is rightly

felt to command their reverence, faith does not fail, hope is not shaken, charity does not grow cold.[11]

One of the principal implied concerns of the apostles at the Ascension was that they would henceforth be without the sustaining presence of Christ. His promise to abide with them somehow after leaving them answered that concern. They did not know until Pentecost the precise form that his presence would take. Meanwhile, as the wonderful reflection of St. Leo makes clear, Jesus' Ascension lifted up to the Father the human nature that had been banished from Paradise by Adam's sin. Because our Intercessor ascended to the Father, a human being—body and soul—represents all other frail and sinful human beings before the heavenly bar of justice. In the divine order, that Intercessor sits at the Father's right hand, above angels and all other created beings. To this great height the Ascension of our Lord carried human nature, in order to restore it fully to grace.

Mary and the Ascension. The Blessed Virgin is among those left behind when Jesus ascended into heaven. We know from her presence with the apostles after the Ascension (Acts 1:14) that she continued to associate with those who had been his closest companions. How close to each other St. John and his newly designated Mother must have been! And how eagerly these two, in the company of the other apostles, must have awaited the fulfillment of the Lord's promise! They didn't know the form the Spirit was to take, but they did know that something of the greatest importance was about to happen. After the little assembly of Christ's intimates became the nascent Church, Mary had but a few years to wait before Jesus called her to himself in the Assumption.

---

[11] *Patrologia Latina* 54, 397; quoted in the *Office of Readings* for Friday of the Sixth Week of Easter.

Meanwhile, Mary believed in him and trusted in his promises as she took part in the sacramental life of the Church, receiving her risen Son in Holy Communion and abiding with him in prayer. After the Ascension, she thus continued to carry out the principle of her vocation—to say "*fiat*" to God's will and to "wait patiently" for the Lord (Psalm 37:7).

Suggested intentions. We may offer this decade of the Rosary in thanksgiving for the Communion of Saints. In the Ascension—the whole act of going to the Father and taking his seat at the Father's right hand—Jesus is surrounded by the host of the saved, who through the grace of God share their spiritual goods with the Church Militant, the Church on earth. As he goes to the Father, Jesus assumes the role of universal Advocate. His intercession does not exclude other intercessory prayer, however, but on the contrary "gives rise to a manifold cooperation which is but a sharing" in himself, the "one source"[12] of grace, Jesus Christ. The Blessed Virgin, the Queen of Saints, is the first in this sharing. She is followed by all the saints throughout the ages, with whom we Christians on earth are in constant communion. Therefore, because in a very real way the Ascension of Christ makes possible the Communion of Saints, let us offer the Ascension decade in thanksgiving to God for that communion and for all it means to us sinners.

---

[12] *Lumen Gentium*, no. 62.

3

THE SENDING OF THE HOLY SPIRIT

Littera: Scripture and gloss. The third great linked event after the death of Christ occurred on the Jewish Feast of Weeks, or Pentecost, and is narrated in the book of Acts:

> Now when the day of Pentecost arrived they were all together in one place. Suddenly a sound like a violent rushing wind came from the sky and filled the whole house where they were staying. Tongues as of fire appeared to them, parting and coming to rest on each of them, and they were all filled with the Holy Spirit and began to speak in different tongues according to how the Spirit inspired them to speak (Acts 2:1-4).

The feast is called the Feast of Weeks because it comes seven weeks and one day after Passover. It is called Pentecost (Greek for "fifty days") because seven weeks and one day equals fifty days. The "all" who were gathered "in one place" included the eleven apostles, the new apostle (Matthias) chosen to take Judas's place, and the Blessed Virgin Mary (cf. Acts 1:14).

Wind is used in the Gospel of St. John as a symbol of the Spirit. Jesus teaches, "The wind blows where it pleases and you hear its voice, but you do not know where it comes from or where it goes. So it is with every one who is born of the Spirit" (John 3:8). The voice of God addresses Job out of a whirlwind (Job 38:1). The word *spirit* itself comes from Latin *spiritus* ("breath"), which comes in turn from *spirare* ("to blow"). It is therefore very appropriate that when the Holy Spirit comes with force upon the followers of Christ, he should be accompanied by the sound of a rushing wind. Fire,

179

used so often in Scripture as a symbol of purification, zeal, and punishment (three theologically connected entities) is here elevated to an eternal symbol of the presence of the Holy Spirit. The candles in ancient times, on our altars today, and beside our tabernacles bespeak the connection. The immediate gift of the Spirit is that of communication—the ability to talk to speakers of foreign languages. Significantly, the "tongues" imparted here by the Spirit are intelligible; they are not babble, and their meaning is not private or subjective.

Further context. The marvelous works of the Spirit on Pentecost are the fulfillment of Christ's promises. As we have seen, before his Ascension he promised the apostles that he would be with them to the end of time (Matthew 28:20). The promise is that he will be with his servants to help them carry out the commission he has just given them, to "make disciples of all the nations" (Matthew 28:18). With the help of the Holy Spirit, sent by Christ, the apostles began to fulfill this commission on that Pentecost.

In St. Mark the promise concerns the power of his *name*, by which the apostles are to work miracles that confirm the Lord's presence. Jesus promises signs that are to

> follow those who believe: they will drive out demons in
> my name; they will speak in new tongues; they will pick
> up snakes in their hands, and if they drink any poison, it
> will not harm them; they will lay their hands on the sick,
> and they will get well (Mark 16:17-18).

Such are the tokens of Christ's presence that marked the ministry of his apostles, who "went forth to proclaim the good news everywhere, the Lord working with them and confirming the word through the signs following upon it" (Mark 16:20). These special emblems of the presence of Christ were notably numerous during the earliest days of the Church, when witnesses to Christ relied for their persuasive power in part upon immediate proofs of his divinity, rather than upon a developed theology or the body of Scripture known as the New Testament, both of which lay in the future. Jesus helped his apostles to be convincing.

A further and related promise that Jesus made to Peter on the Mount of the Transfiguration (Matthew 16:19: "I will give you the keys of the Kingdom") begins its fulfillment on Pentecost when Peter for the first time boldly asserts his leadership. In fact, the descent of the Holy Spirit gives St. Peter the power and authority symbolized by the keys. The successor of St. Peter, the bishop of Rome, and the bishops in union with him retain this authority. I have mentioned that many passages of the New Testament quietly emphasize the primacy of Peter. Peter's role as vicar of Christ, the Son of God and Chief Pastor, is again strongly emphasized at the end of the Gospel of St. John (21:15-19). The Lord asked him three times, "Peter, do you love me?" and Peter, with three increasingly strong protestations of love, said "Yes, yes, *yes*." After each affirmation, Jesus instructed him, "Feed my sheep"—words that explicitly commission a *pastor* or shepherd. As this commission was addressed to no one else, it had to mean that St. Peter was being made the Good Shepherd's shepherd—the vicar who was to remain in Christ's absence: the head, that is, of the apostle-bishops and consequently of the hierarchy of the Church.

Extensions and applications. There is no question that Peter was the leading recipient of the Pentecost promise, for after the immediate reactions of the crowd it was he who stood and spoke for all the apostles (Acts 2:14-42). He was, as it were, the official spokesman who told the gathering multitude the meaning of the startling events they had witnessed. Peter pointed out that Jesus is the fulfillment of the ancient prophecy to David, as the Joyful Mysteries teach. He made it clear that his colleagues were not drunk, as some charged, but that the signs they were beginning to manifest (the first of which was speaking in tongues) were possible only because Jesus Christ was still somehow with them. The signs, or miracles, were the salient proof of a supernatural presence. And when St. Peter identified that presence as the very Jesus whom the crowd had caused to be crucified, his auditors were "pierced to the heart" and asked what they could do to be saved. "About three thousand" were baptized on Pentecost, presumably including some of those who conspired in the Lord's death. Thus the beginning of the Church was the answer to Christ's prayer from the cross that his tormentors might be forgiven (Luke 23:34).

Pentecost is also the climactic event in the transformation of the apostles. If the Crucifixion was the nadir of their career, when they thought all was lost; if the Resurrection gave them a new but ill-defined hope that was sustained through the Ascension only by faith in the one who promised; then the Descent of the Holy Spirit at Pentecost gave them strength and courage, told them what to do, and helped them to be steadfast in doing it. The Comforter, or Paraclete,[13] became operative in the absence of Christ—according to the promise—and thus worked miracles for St. Peter and his companions.

Often—too often, it seems to me—homilies emphasize the "cowardice" and "betrayal" of St. Peter at the Crucifixion. Preachers concentrate upon the earlier failures of this first pope and ignore his later career, when he was a paragon of courage and pastoral leadership. At the Crucifixion he was already stronger than most of the disciples, who had disappeared; in the crowd that hung around waiting for the end of Christ's trial, Peter was overcome by the same kind of instinctive fear for his life that every honest man must see in himself. It was the triad of Resurrection - Ascension - Pentecost that made the new St. Peter. The coming of the Holy Spirit wiped out the last traces of fear and bewilderment among the apostles, including their leader.

---

[13] The word *Paraclete*, which means "Advocate," is often translated "Comforter." The point of the latter translation is that the Holy Spirit will comfort the people of God in the absence of the Son.

Under the guidance of the Holy Spirit, the sacramental activity of the Church began on Pentecost. Thus the Church's identity was from the very beginning inseparable from her mediation of Christ to the world through the sacraments. Those three thousand recipients of the sacrament of Baptism represent the first of the human race to receive Christ as presented sacramentally through his Mystical Body. This is what the Holy Spirit caused to occur that day: he brought a body of human beings together and made them into the Body of Christ, the sacrament of salvation. By the Lord's own action through his ministers, the water of Baptism washed away the sins of those who had crucified him, and the recipients of this sacrament became new members of the infant Church. These first members of the Church are thus prototypes of all to whom Christ draws near through the Eucharist, Baptism, Confession, Confirmation, Holy Orders, the Anointing of the Sick, and Holy Matrimony. The wonderful presence of Jesus Christ himself is guaranteed to his Church in all ages, as the ministers of his sacraments (including husbands and wives, who are ministers of the sacrament of matrimony) bring him to those who desire to receive him.

The Holy Spirit had descended upon Christ at his baptism (Mark 1:10) in the iconic form by which he is best known—that of a dove. Previously, throughout the history of man, the Spirit had been involved in creation and in God's self-revelation to his people, though no clear idea of God's manifestation in a third Person had been developed. The Old Testament writers wrote under the inspiration of the Holy Spirit just as surely as did the evangelists. But the concept of the Trinity awaited the full revelation of the Son and then the Holy Spirit. On the day of Pentecost Jesus fulfilled in a spectacular way his promise to *be with* the apostles, and he showed them how he was going to do this—through perpetually sending the Spirit. It behooved the Son to ascend first to the Father, so that on Pentecost the Holy Spirit could be sent forth from the Father and the Son.

After Pentecost it became increasingly clear that the *spiritual* presence of God—this Holy Spirit—was what had been promised. From then on, Jesus the Son of Man was to be present through his Spirit, and the Father was to be present with them both; for the Persons of the Blessed Trinity, though distinct, are inseparable. Henceforth the loyal children of Holy Mother Church would recognize the presence of the Holy Spirit in the Church's Magisterium. They would also know, with St. Paul, that the Holy Spirit is the individual Christian's Advocate, who complements our prayers perfectly with inexpressible groanings, "sighs too deep for words" (Romans 8:26), which perfect our weak efforts and lift them up to the Lord. The Holy Spirit, as our Advocate, addresses the Father as we would address him if we were not fallen. After Pentecost, it became clear that God the Holy Spirit is the source of all good impulses that come to human creatures—such impulses as inspire the sacred writings and help us followers of Christ to war against spiritual death. Henceforward, Christ himself, in the person of his priests, would invoke the Holy Spirit to rush upon the altars of the faithful and transform the humble gifts of bread and wine into his own Body and Blood for the nourishment of his people. He thus again sends the Spirit, and again and again. The "gifts of the Holy Spirit"[14] had always been available to those who sought them, but after Pentecost their origin became clear. So much was revealed on that day!

Mary on Pentecost. Our Lady was habitually with the apostles after the Resurrection, as Acts 1:12-14 makes clear. Pope Paul VI pointed out that "the last description of Mary's life presents her as praying. The apostles 'joined in continuous prayer, together with several women, including Mary the mother of Jesus' (Acts 1:14). We have here the prayerful presence of Mary in the early Church."[15]

---

[14] Galatians 5:22-23: "The fruit of the Spirit is love, joy, peace, patience, kindness, goodness, faithfulness, gentleness, self-control."

[15] Pope Paul VI, *Marialis Cultus*, February 2, 1974, no. 18.

On the day of Pentecost she was there to share the exhilaration, the spiritual vindication, the glory of the occasion. *But she was already filled by the Holy Spirit.* She herself had been voluntarily "overshadowed" by him at the Annunciation. The habit of her life was to be his temple. Now, after the dark days of the Crucifixion and the mysterious promises associated with the Ascension, she shares the power and the glory that comes upon the apostles. The Holy Spirit is therefore always with our Blessed Mother. When we seek her, we seek him. When she guides us, he guides us. When we give our lives and wills to Mary, we put ourselves in the hands of God.

Suggested intentions. From the time that the Blessed Virgin said "Be it done to me according to your word," it was clear that she had given her life and her will to God completely. We should pray to do the same: that we will be entirely open to the guidance of the Holy Spirit but to nothing else. For following the Spirit's guidance entails obedience to the teachings of the Church and to our consciences as they are informed and led by these teachings. It entails daily prayer and contemplation. It entails a daily search for knowledge of the will of God and the grace to carry it out, and so to fulfill our vocation in Christ. It entails awareness of the presence of the Blessed Virgin, for the Holy Spirit is always with her. It does *not*, however, entail "openness" to sin, or to rebellion against Christ's Church.

We should always make the prayer to the Holy Spirit ours:

Come, Holy Spirit,
fill the hearts of thy faithful
and kindle in them the fire of thy love.

When our lives are in perfect harmony with this prayer—a lofty goal—we will love God with all our hearts and our neighbor as ourselves. And we will remain securely within the fold of Christ's Church.

4

THE ASSUMPTION
OF THE BLESSED VIRGIN MARY

Littera and gloss. The Assumption and Coronation of the Blessed Virgin continue the submission that the Son shows to his Mother on earth, for these mysteries express his filial desire to honor her, just as he obeyed her when he was a child. Remember, too, the wedding at Cana, where Jesus performed his first miracle. It clearly demonstrates this desire. The Lord is expressly not yet ready to begin his public ministry: "My hour has not come," he tells her (John 1:4). And yet, at her bidding, he turns the water to wine. So great is Mary's maternal influence on her Son that we should never forget it, but should turn it to our benefit. We should go "to Jesus through Mary," as the popular phrase has it. *This is what the wedding guests did.* On her part, Mary's admonition to "Do whatever he tells you" (John 1:5) expresses a faith in Jesus that grows in her through the years and leads ultimately to her Assumption into heaven and her Coronation.

The literal texts for the Assumption and the Coronation are of a different order from those passages that report the other mysteries. Scriptural references to the Blessed Virgin Mary in heaven are few and symbolic, not direct and literal. In fact, most Marian theology elaborates on scriptural suggestions and logical necessities gradually perceived, not on extensive or explicit scriptural statements. The Church's teaching on Mary's triumph comes from scriptural hints as elaborated in Sacred Tradition. The teaching is a compelling, natural, organic outgrowth of this Spirit-led Catholic meditation on Scripture and the Incarnation of Christ. Though glimpsed only briefly in Scripture, the Mary of Catholic faith is the Mary that has to be.

The woman who gives birth to the Lamb in Revelation 12 symbolizes both Israel and, just as importantly, the Virgin Mary. As the representative of Israel who gave birth to the Lamb of God, Mary is the actual agent who brings the New Covenant to fruition. The woman in Revelation wears a crown of twelve stars. Israel comprised twelve tribes, and accordingly Jesus chose twelve apostles. Whether the author of Revelation primarily intended the woman figure to represent Israel or Mary or the Church, Mary is still necessarily the focal point, for she is the historical Mother of the Son symbolized by the Lamb. The passage is well known:

> Then a great sign was seen in the sky—a woman clothed with the sun, with the moon beneath her feet, and a crown of twelve stars on her head. She was pregnant and was crying out in the pangs of childbirth (Revelation 12:1-2).

In the cosmic warfare that ensued, St. Michael the Archangel defeated the red dragon, "that ancient serpent, who is called the Devil and Satan, who deceived the whole world" (Revelation 12:9), and cast him down to earth. After the heavenly battle, the deceiver turned upon "the woman who had given birth to the male child." Unable to destroy her, he "went off to wage war on the rest of her offspring—those who keep God's commandments and accept the testimony of Jesus" (Revelation 12:13,17). Subsequently, those who conquer the dragon do so "through the blood of the Lamb and through the word of their testimony" (Revelation 12:11); that is, by their bearing witness to Christ even if it means their death.

The Church has constantly deepened her understanding of the Blessed Virgin's role in salvation history. In this inspired thought process, the understanding of Our Lady's Immaculate

Conception led necessarily to the Assumption. She *had* to be conceived without sin so that she would be a fitting Mother to the Son of God. Because of this Immaculate Conception, she was necessarily exempt from the corruption of death common to those who have sinned. Pope Pius XII remarked that "the two dogmas are intimately connected in close bond." They are based on "two very singular privileges bestowed upon the Virgin Mother of God ... as the beginning and as the end of her earthly journey; for the greatest possible glorification of her virgin body is the complement, at once appropriate and marvelous, of the absolute innocence of her soul, which was free from all stain."[16]

This centuries-old perception, which developed organically from Scripture and was expressed throughout the history of the Church, brought the Holy Father in 1950 to define the dogma of the Assumption:

> After We have unceasingly offered Our most fervent prayers to God, and have called upon the Spirit of Truth, for the glory of Almighty God who has lavished his special affection upon the Virgin Mary, for the honor of her Son, the immortal King of the Ages and the Victor over sin and death, for the increase of the glory of that same august Mother, and for the joy and exultation of the entire Church; by the authority of our Lord Jesus Christ, of the blessed Apostles Peter and Paul, and by Our own authority, *We pronounce, declare, and define it to be a divinely revealed dogma: that the Immaculate Mother of God, the ever Virgin Mary, having completed the course of her earthly life, was assumed body and soul into heavenly glory.*
>
> Hence if anyone ... should dare wilfully to deny or to call into doubt that which we have defined, let him know

---

[16] Pope Pius XII, *Fulgens Corona*, September 8, 1953, nos. 20 and 21.

that he has fallen away completely from the divine and Catholic Faith.[17]

Further context. The divine rationale behind the Assumption—as far as divine rationales are available to human understanding—is contained in this papal pronouncement. The Assumption was but *one* glorious step in a series of instances in which "Almighty God ... lavished his special affection upon the Virgin Mary, for the honor of her Son." It also redounded "to the glory of that same august Mother, and [to] the joy and exultation of the entire Church."

We have seen the affection of God for Mary throughout the mysteries of the Rosary. It begins in the Annunciation and continues through the rest of the Joyful Mysteries. It finds painful expression in the Sorrowful Mysteries, where the vocation to proceed from joy to glory leads through the dark valley of great suffering. God scourges every son that he loves. The Virgin's high calling and the sorrow through which it leads her are ample witness that he also scourges his daughters. Daughter Israel, Mary the special Daughter of Israel, and every other obedient daughter of the heavenly Father must also bear whips and reversals before attaining glory. For both daughters and sons, the cross precedes resurrection. Such is the demanding mercy of God.

After the dark valley—the apparent defeat of Calvary—come the first three Glorious Mysteries, the Resurrection, the Ascension, and the Descent of the Holy Spirit. In these the Blessed Virgin receives glory vicariously, through her Son—just as in the Sorrowful Mysteries she has undergone unspeakable vicarious suffering in empathy with Jesus. But in the last two mysteries, the Assumption

---

[17] Pope Pius XII, *Munificentissimus Deus*, November 2, 1950.

and the Coronation, Our Lady is *directly* glorified. This fact detracts not at all from Jesus, for the Assumption glorifies Mary's Son as well and makes him and his Church rejoice. It does so precisely because in these last Glorious Mysteries God shows that he "rewards those who seek him" (Hebrews 11:6). God especially honors Mary for her faithfulness in fulfilling his will.

Extensions and applications. Early in his earthly life, when he first became able to act responsibly in a human sense, Jesus became obedient to Mary. Thus in his Incarnation and in continuing to live his human life, God abased himself before his own creation. But by the grace of God his creature Mary, immaculate in her conception, lived in such a way as to *merit* honor from the Lord himself. Without a quibble, she cooperated with the Father by bringing the Son into the world. The Son, for his part, though eternally perfect in himself, humbled himself to have human needs. In perfect sinlessness, in perfect self-giving, the Virgin Mother gave the growing boy all he needed, though her life with him was not without pain. For her self-gift to him the Lord honored Mary in his life. Then, at the end of her earthly sojourn, he honored her supremely and rewarded her for her great faithfulness by calling her to his side in heaven.

In her life Mary was the perfect model of the Church because of her obedient cooperation with the Father and the Son. As a result, she became the prototype of the victorious Christian, who will be caught up to heaven at the last judgment. When he ascended into heaven Jesus lifted our human nature up to the Father and restored it to its original glory. In his heavenly role as intercessor, judge, and rewarder of his servants, he lifted his Mother, the first Christian, to the glory of heaven. Mary thus became the recipient, like Christ himself, of the promise that God will not let "his godly one see the pit" of death (Psalm 16:10). We, all of us corrupted by sin, must await the last day for our resurrection and reward. But we can see in the Assumption what awaits us if we are deemed worthy, through Christ's grace, of sharing the Virgin's glory in heaven.

Mary in the glory of the Assumption. Catholics are often accused of "idolatry" of one form or another: of "worshiping statues" or "praying to people." Once, in a sort of ecumenical mood, a Protestant said to me, "Yes, I believe in the Communion of Saints, but I don't see what's so special about Mary." The answer is that *God* considered her special. The Son *chose* Mary as the one to bear him into the world. He *created* her for this purpose. Because he could not be borne by a sinful vessel he created her free of original sin. He then honored her as his Mother. He obeyed her dutifully and saw to her needs while he was dying. Thus, in all his earthly life and even before it, Jesus honored Mary above all other human beings. *That* makes her special. Her Assumption, a spectacular continuation of that honor, invites us to honor her, too, in imitation of Jesus. Let us do so with all our hearts. "In the Assumption [we] recognize the beginning that has already been made and the image of what, for the whole Church, must still come to pass. In the mystery of Mary's motherhood [we] confess that she is the Mother of the Head and of the members—the holy Mother of God and therefore the provident Mother of the Church."[18]

Suggested intentions. The great reward of the Assumption did not come automatically to the Blessed Virgin. By God's grace and her cooperation with it, she *earned* it. She is therefore the measure of true righteousness. Through the grace of her Son, she

---

[18] Pope Paul VI, *Marialis Cultus*, no. 11.

is also the Mother of all human beings. We should pray that she will help us to be the kind of righteous children she wants us to be, and that Jesus will help us to imitate him by honoring her. With her help "we can portray" in our lives some small part of her fidelity "to all God's designs" and as a reward "follow her into heaven."[19]

---

[19] Pope Leo XIII, *Magnae Dei Matris*, September 8, 1892, no. 26.

5

THE CORONATION
OF THE BLESSED VIRGIN

Littera and gloss. The Coronation is inseparably related to the Assumption. The "Immaculate Virgin, preserved free from all stain of original sin, was taken up body and soul into heavenly glory when her life was over, and exalted by the Lord as Queen over all things, that she might be the more fully conformed to her Son, the Lord of lords and conqueror of sin and death."[20] The taking up and the exaltation are two parts of the same process, that of rewarding Mary for her faithfulness and making her the model for all Christians. We look to her as the "model of virtues" who "prompts the faithful to come to her Son."[21]

But Mary is more than a model. Just as Jesus is more than an example for our emulation, the Blessed Virgin embodies a perfection to which we can only aspire. According to the Holy Father, she has reached "a height of glory granted to no other creature, whether human or angelic." As "the invincible Queen of Martyrs," she sits in the "heavenly city of God by the side of her Son, crowned for all eternity."[22] The reward that we seek for our devotion to God's will is analogous to the honors that Mary receives. But our righteousness and purity must always be at best a poor shadow of hers. All the more reason for us to strive for perfection.

---

[20] *Lumen Gentium*, no. 59, notes omitted.

[21] *Ibid.*, no. 65.

[22] Pope Leo XIII, *Magnae Dei Matris*, no. 25.

Pope Pius XII instituted celebration of the Queenship of Mary as a liturgical feast. In his document devoted to this purpose,[23] he points to the antiquity of Mary's title as Queen, just as he had noted the ancient tradition of the Assumption. Mary's universal motherhood is tied up with her royal reign: "Mary, the Virgin Mother of God, reigns with a mother's solicitude over the entire world, just as she is crowned in heavenly blessedness with the glory of a Queen." Many fathers and doctors of the Church had given her queenly dignity and royal titles—"Queen of all creatures, the Queen of the world, and the Ruler of all."

As I have stated, Mary's dignity is not original with her. It is derived, like all human dignity, from God—who is her Son. In her role as Queen, Mary is the antitype of the original queen of the race, Eve. In faithfully fulfilling her vocation as the "handmaid of the Lord," Mary restores what Eve lost by disobedience. In her maternal role, Mary is the Mother to whom the downtrodden and suffering of the earth can look for help. The Holy Father exhorts: "Let all Christians, therefore, glory in being *subjects* of the Virgin Mother of God, who, while wielding royal power, is on fire with a mother's love" (emphasis added).

Further context. Jesus was prophet, priest, and king, and all Christians are to share these roles with the Lord. The proper sign of kingship, a crown, appears frequently in Scripture as a mark of honor, especially in the context of Judgment Day. Followers of Christ who by his grace overcome the world and attain to everlasting life are to receive a reward symbolized by a crown. St. Paul writes to St. Timothy,

---

[23] Pope Pius XII, *Ad Caeli Reginam: On Proclaiming the Queenship of Mary*, October 11, 1954. Quotations in this paragraph and the next are from this document.

I have fought the good fight, I have finished the race, I have kept the faith. From here on the crown of righteousness is being laid aside for me, which the Lord, the just judge, will award me on that Day, and not only me but all those who have longed for his appearing (2 Timothy 4:7-8).

St. James writes, "Happy is the man who is steadfast in temptation! When he has been proved worthy he will receive the crown of life that God has promised to those who love him" (James 1:12). In fulfilling his role as the vicar of Christ by exhorting the shepherds of the Church to faithfulness, St. Peter promises, "when the chief Shepherd is revealed you will receive an unfading crown of glory" (1 Peter 5:4). The crown reserved for the "good and faithful" (Matthew 25:21) servants of God is therefore associated with righteousness or right living, with endurance under trial, and with faithful discharge of pastoral duty. With it come life and glory. It seems inevitable that the Blessed Virgin, who preeminently lived a life of faith and righteousness, would receive a reward symbolized by a coronation in heaven. For this Christ called her to his side.

Extensions and applications. Just as figures in the Old Testament—Moses, for instance—were types, or foreshadowing images, of Christ, through her exaltation the Blessed Virgin becomes a type—or foreshadowing symbol— of both the Church victorious and of the individual Christian who through Christ gains eternal life. "As St. Ambrose taught, the Mother of God is a type of the Church in the order of faith, charity, and perfect union with Christ."[24]

The Coronation is figurative, of course, though the Assumption is not. Although the language used for the removal or elevation of the Blessed Virgin from earth to heaven is necessarily

---

[24] *Lumen Gentium*, no. 63, note omitted.

figurative, the event signified by it actually occurred. Mary was spiritually, and somehow physically, exalted into the eternal presence of her Son. The Coronation, however, is a purely figurative construct derived from the fact that a queen is honored above all other women. The language of honor to a royal lady is perhaps the most appropriate language to use for the Blessed Virgin. And the Coronation has brought forth countless beautiful works of art, all manifestations of a divine gift and all dedicated to the Mother of Jesus, our Queen.

Jesus is a King of a different order from other kings. He rules over a realm that "is not of this world" (John 18:36), and his methods of rule are self-sacrifice, justice, mercy—all the attributes of real love, which comes from God. Oddly for a king, Jesus "came not to be served but to serve, and to give his life as a ransom for many" (Matthew 20:28). Accordingly, the Blessed Virgin Mary rules by conforming to the model of her Son. She is no haughty ruler but a Sovereign of maternal love. Her methods of rule are "mercy, pity, peace, and love," to appropriate words of the poet William Blake.[25] It is the Catholic belief that Mary is always with Jesus, interceding for all her children.

This intercession, as I have said, enhances the role of Christ rather than detracting from it.

> The Blessed Virgin's salutary influence on men originates ... in the disposition of God. It flows forth from the superabundance of the merits of Christ, rests on his mediation, depends entirely on it and draws all its power from it. It does not hinder in any way the immediate union of the faithful with Christ but on the contrary fosters it.[26]

---

[25] William Blake, *Songs of Innocence.* Blake was not talking about the Blessed Virgin, but about the true face of man in the unfallen state.

[26] *Lumen Gentium,* no. 60.

"Hail Mary, full of Grace! The Lord is *with* thee" we pray. Draw near to Mary and you draw near to Christ. Attacks on the Catholic Church often assume the form of attacks on our honoring Mary. It is true that some Catholics have imagined an opposition between Jesus and Mary, but the Church herself has never agreed. What the Church has taught is that Mary is above all other saints and consequently deserves a higher degree of honor. The worship of Divinity belongs to God alone.[27] That limitation accords perfectly with the will of Mary herself, whose scanty life record in Scripture reveals not a glory-seeker but the humble "handmaid of the Lord."

Mary, the Queen of Heaven. Mary's heavenly Queenship is a natural extension of her life on earth, where her Son honored her, obeyed her, allowed her to open his public ministry, and cared for her with filial love from the cross. In her faithfulness she abides with the apostles, witnesses the miracles of Pentecost, and at her death receives Jesus' call to join him in heaven. The Coronation is a simple continuation: as he had made her Queen of his life, he makes her Queen of Heaven.

Suggested intentions. Jesus lifted Mary from the human condition of death and corruption and crowned her Queen of heaven and earth, Queen of his Church. In accord with our duty to mirror Christ in our lives, we should honor his Mother as he did. Let us therefore pray for the reign of the Blessed Virgin in our lives. For when she rules in our hearts, he will rule. As we honor her, we honor him. When we are her subjects, we are truly subjects of Christ—his brothers and sisters and heirs of his kingdom.

---

[27] See *Lumen Gentium*, nos. 66, 67.

Afterword

THE ROSARY AS A LIVING PRAYER

$\mathcal{T}$he Rosary can become a living prayer for you. One of my intentions in this book has been to show how it can develop from an often mechanical and monotonous devotion, cut off from the world around us, to a vital and unifying part of one's daily prayer. The Rosary can give increased meaning and coherence to all of your prayer life, since the mysteries contain within themselves a means of moving toward an integral spiritual life through scriptural reflection. Pope Paul VI calls the Rosary an "epitome of the whole Gospel," a phrase quoted in the *Catechism of the Catholic Church* (971).[1] That means that praying the Rosary can make the Gospel a vital part of your daily thinking, hence an element of conversion.

But it doesn't stop with you. Application of the mysteries to various aspects of modern culture grows naturally into socially directed prayers of petition. Scriptural reflection—and reflection on how the Mysteries relate to the joys, pains, and glories of the world around us—can make us voices of prayer and instruments of grace to a world in need. Scriptural reflection deepens our understanding of others—of their spiritual needs—particularly in our increasingly secular culture, which *needs* our prayers. I have tried to show

---

[1] Pope Paul VI, *Marialis Cultus* (February 2, 1974), no. 42; *Catechism of the Catholic Church*, no. 971.

201

how this can take place by suggesting how appropriate various parts of the Rosary are as offerings for specific intentions. My own experience has convinced me of the value of this process. Increased contemplation of the Mysteries reveals their universal applications to the human situation.

We live in a fragmenting world. Corrosive philosophies that elevate doubt above faith, that attack Christian tradition, and that deny the very existence of truth have gained the upper hand in many intellectual circles. Now, even more than when T.S. Eliot characterized the modern era as a "waste land," we live in a "heap of broken images."[2] In her role as a worldwide "sign of contradiction," the Catholic Church still proclaims the truth to a world thirsty for it. She proclaims that God exists, that he has revealed himself to man, that through his Son he has brought redemption to the human race. The Church rightly teaches what man intuitively knows but popularly denies—that goodness is an objective reality, a truth that exists independent of man's perceptions, and that faith, hope, and love are still the supreme motives behind all that is good. The Church holds out to us the age-old knowledge that the Scriptures are an integral product of divine guidance, marked, to be sure, by the human intellect, but nevertheless unified and wholly reliable in their teaching, which often transcends the intentions of the human authors.

The mysteries of the Rosary partake of this unity and reinforce it. These great scenes from the life of Christ and the Blessed Virgin are the central matter of the New Testament. They are rich with meanings from the Old Testament. They resound in the life of the early Church, and their profound spiritual music has brought harmony in the soul of the Church through the ages. These facts

---

[2] T.S. Eliot, *The Waste Land*, line 22.

should lead us to perceive new connections between the mysteries and our own lives. If they do, we will be supremely enriched. For the great meditative heritage of the Church is a luminous record of such perceptions.

This book was designed and published by St. Pauls/ Alba House, the publishing arm of the Society of St. Paul, an international religious congregation of priests and brothers dedicated to serving the Church through the communications media. For information regarding this and associated ministries of the Pauline Family of Congregations, write to the Vocation Director, Society of St. Paul, 7050 Pinehurst, Dearborn, Michigan 48126. Phone (313) 582-3798 or check our internet site, www.albahouse.org